This is the first of a series of books on the performance of classical music being prepared under the general editorship of Oscar Shoenfeld.

*Titles in this series include:*
Sonatas for Violin and Piano *by Abram Loft*
Chamber Music for Wind Instruments *by Samuel Baron*
The Performance of Baroque Music *by Victor Rangel-Ribeiro*

786·2

The Piano Duet

33030

Mozart with his sister Nannerl and father Leopold (oil painting by della Croce).

# THE PIANO DUET

*A Guide for Pianists*

*by* ERNEST LUBIN

**A DA CAPO PAPERBACK**

Library of Congress Cataloging in Publication Data

Lubin, Ernest.
  The piano duet.

  (A Da Capo paperback)
  Reprint of the ed. published by Grossman, New
York.
  Includes bibliographical references.
  1. Piano music (4 hands) — History and criticism.
I. Title.
  [ML700.L82 1976]        786.4'04'1    76-10328
  ISBN 0-306-88045-4

ISBN 0-306-80045-4

First Paperback Printing 1976

This Da Capo Paperback edition of *The Piano Duet*
is an unabridged republication of the first edition
published in New York in 1970. It is reprinted
by arrangement with Grossman Publishers.

Published by Da Capo Press, Inc.
A Subsidiary of Plenum Publishing Corporation
227 West 17th Street
New York, N.Y. 10011

Grateful acknowledgment is made to the following publishers of copyright music used in the text:

G. Schirmer, Inc., New York, for Samuel Barber's "Souvenirs."

Weintraub Music Company, New York, for Robert Kurka's "Dance Suite."

J. & W. Chester, Ltd., London, for Poulenc's "Sonata," Berners' "Trois Valses Bourgeoises" and Casella's "Puppazetti."

Durand & Cie., Paris, for Debussy's "Epigraphes Antiques," Ravel's "Ma mere l'oye," Andre Caplet's "Un tas de petites choses" and Florent Schmitt's "Une semaine du petit elfe Ferme l'oieul."

Editions Cosallat, 60 Rue de la Chaussee d'Antin, Paris, for the "Souvenirs de Munich" of Chabrier and the "Souvenirs de Bayreuth" of Faure and Messager.

B. Schott's Sohne, Mainz, for the Hindemith Sonata and the Dawes' edition of "Two Elizabethan Duets." Used by permission of Belwin-Mills Music Corp., Rockville Center, New York.

Theodore Presser Co., Bryn Mawr, Pa., for Schumann's Polonaises, opus III. Copyright by Universal Edition, Vienna.

Associated Music Publishers for Respighi's "Six Pieces for Piano Duet." Copyright 1926 by N. Simrock.

Polskie Wydawnictwo Muzyczne, Krakow, Poland, for Chopin's "Variations on a National Air of Thomas Moore."

Douglas Townsend of New York for Donizetti's "Sonata" and J. C. Bach's "Little Sonata in C."

Thanks are due also to *Clavier* and to *The American Music Teacher* for permission to reprint sections of this book that first appeared in their pages.

# 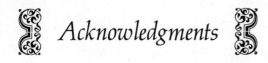 Acknowledgments

Every book is in some degree a collaboration, and this book more than most others has depended on the help and cooperation of many people.

First and foremost I am indebted to my old friend, now my editor, Oscar Shoenfeld. It was in a conversation with him some years ago that the idea for this book first germinated, and without his active and enlightened interest, support, advice, encouragement and prodding, it is very doubtful that this book would ever have been written.

I owe a very particular debt of gratitude to two friends and colleagues of many years' standing, Ted Dalbotten and Douglas Townsend, both of whom have shared with me their truly extraordinary libraries of four-hand music, which to a remarkable degree have supplemented each other. Mr. Dalbotten's collection includes all the standard and many far from standard works, and for many years, even before this book was ever thought of, I have had the pleasure of playing and working with him. Mr. Townsend is well known as an imaginative and enterprising musicologist, and his four-hand collection is especially rich in rare and unusual items that he has gathered from all corners of the world. Among the works discussed in this book that I have had the opportunity of seeing through his generosity are sonatas by Jomelli, Johann Christian Bach, Dussek and Donizetti, the "lessons" of J. C. Bach, the duet concerto of Czerny, and other interesting and unusual things by Clementi, Franz Duschek and Rossini. I am also grateful to Mr. Townsend for reading the second and sixth, and to Mr. Dalbotten for reading the eighth chapter of this book in typescript and for offering valuable suggestions.

It would be impossible to mention all the friends who have helped make this book possible by playing duets with me, but I should like to offer a special word of thanks to Constance Keene, Joseph Wolman, Jay Gottlieb, Paul Spong, Alice and Morris Lawner and Audrey and Murray Lane.

Among music dealers who have been helpful in obtaining duet material, I should particularly like to thank Mr. Victor Rangel-Ribiero of the Orpheus Music Shop in New York as well as the friendly and helpful staff of the Patelson Music Shop and Schirmer's in New York and the Dale Music Shop in Silver Springs, Maryland. Much of the material discussed in this book is available only in libraries, and I am grateful to Mr. Jon Newsom of the Music Division of the Library of Congress in Washington, Mr. Oliver Nieghbour of the Music Room of the British Museum, Miss Natalie McCance of the Royal College of Music, and to the staff of the Music Library in New York, the Boston Public Library, the Newberry Library in Chicago and the Columbia University Library for many valuable items.

Among the many individuals who have provided music or information that I could not have obtained otherwise, I am grateful to Humphrey Searle for data about the Liszt catalogue, to Raymond Lewenthal for Alkan duets, to Mrs. Alison Nelson Neal for the two-piano version of the Mendelssohn-Moscheles variations, and to Joan and Kenneth Wentworth, Peggy and Milton Salkind, John Duke, Frank Cooper, Ray Green, William Goldberg, Lillian Primack, Cameron McGraw and David Goldberger. A word of thanks also to Pamela Roma for her poetic interpretation of the Pavane from Ravel's "Mother Goose Suite." Among those who have offered help in many other ways in the preparation of this book I should like to thank George Casseen, Milton Hindus, Rhoda Abrams, Bella Malinka, Dr. Rachel Yocum and my sister Mrs. Renée Gallop.

And last, but most certainly not least, my appreciation to my wife, Eleanore, and my children, Miriam, Robert and Daniel, for putting up with the inevitable and endless inconvenience and sacrifice necessitated by my involvement with this book.

 *Preface*

Since this book is intended primarily for practical musicians and music lovers who wish to explore a neglected area of musical literature, the body of the text is devoted for the main part to compositions of genuine musical interest that are presently in print. For the sake of completeness, however, we have reserved the appendix for discussion of works of historical interest that may no longer be available, and it is hoped that every work of any importance for piano duet will be at least mentioned. But in spite of every effort, there will no doubt be some inadvertent omissions, and the author will be gateful to readers who may be able to offer additions or corrections for use in possible future editions.

# Contents

# The Piano Duet

# I ⚜ *Introduction*

CERTAINLY one of the most curious and fascinating episodes in the history of music is the rise and decline of the art of the piano duet. This very special form of chamber music in which two players perform at the same keyboard hardly even existed before the introduction of the piano in the latter part of the eighteenth century. Then beginning with a trickle of piano duet compositions by Mozart and his contemporaries, it became by Schubert's time a flowing stream, and before much longer a tidal wave that inundated the entire musical life of the nineteenth century.

Shortly after the end of the century the tide receded almost as suddenly as it had arisen, leaving in its wake a mass of flotsam and jetsam in the form of innumerable salon pieces and arrangements. But along with them are hidden pearls of rare beauty that remain enveloped in the almost complete oblivion that has overtaken the entire piano duet repertory. In this age of musical rediscovery when even the most trifling composers of the Baroque era have been able to attain a respectable place in the Schwann catalogue of recorded music, perhaps the time may have come at last to take another look at some of the neglected masterpieces for piano duet.

Let us begin by defining the scope of this work. It is primarily a survey of the music composed expressly for the medium of the piano duet by the great masters from Mozart to Debussy who have made this form their own. Nor shall we overlook a number of minor masters who have also enriched the repertory. However we are not concerned here with arrangements for piano duet of works composed for other mediums, a classification which comprises such a large share of the published output for piano duet. Tovey has remarked somewhere that if you ask a musical amateur what he knows for piano duet he is likely to answer, "Well, Haydn's symphonies." Haydn's symphonies, or any other symphonies arranged for piano duet are most emphatically not piano duet music, any more than Haydn's symphonies arranged for piano solo are piano music. Occasionally we may make an exception for piano duet arrangements that possess some feature of special interest, such as Beethoven's own arrangement for piano duet of his "Grosse Fuge," but these are clearly special cases.

Nor are we concerned here with the literature for two pianos, although this too is a fascinating province for study; a province, incidentally, which has been most capably surveyed in Hans Moldenhauer's excellent book entitled *Duo Pianism.** Anyone who has played both piano duets and two-piano music must have been struck by the difference in style and character between the two mediums. The two piano form allows a greater freedom and independence to each of the players, while the proximity of two pianists at the same keyboard leads in the piano duet to a closer sympathy and interplay between the partners. Naturally the difference between the two mediums is reflected in the music composed for them; while two-piano music tends toward a greater virtuosity, the piano duet leans rather toward a chamber music style.

This book, then, is concerned with the small but wonderful literature, now so largely neglected, of music conceived and written for the piano duet, a literature that flowered mainly during the limited period from the end of the eighteenth century to the beginning of the twentieth.

It may be interesting for a moment to inquire into the reasons for the largely nineteenth-century character of the piano duet. The keyboard instruments in use before the introduction of the piano, such as the harpsichord and clavichord, were too small in size to easily accommodate two performers at one keyboard, and their tone was,

* Chicago Musical College Press, 1950.

moreover, too small to particularly benefit from any multiplication of the notes played. Even two players could hardly have increased the volume to any appreciable extent. And in any case the relatively delicate contrapuntal style of an earlier period would have hardly suggested the need for more than one player to do it justice. But the piano, with its increased range and power and with the added resonance of the pedal, provided the opportunity for a greatly increased sonority with the introduction of a second player. And the more dramatic and homophonic style of the nineteenth century was able to take the fullest advantage of the added possibilities thus provided for doubling of parts and reinforcement of volume.

Once there was an artistic justification for the new medium of the piano duet, there soon came to be an equally potent social justification for it. We cannot easily imagine, with our twentieth-century freedom of social convention, how much more limited social opportunities were in the nineteenth century. But the piano duet provided an acceptable way for young people, particularly of opposite sexes, to come together. Perhaps it is more than a mere accident that so much piano duet music involves a crossing of the hands between the partners, even where it may not be absolutely required by the music itself. Readers of Grieg's biography may perhaps remember how he and his cousin first discovered that they loved each other while playing a piano duet arrangement of Schumann's *Spring Symphony*; and it would be hazardous to venture a guess as to how many nineteenth-century marriages owed their existence to the custom of playing piano duets.

With the more liberal social climate of our own time, much of the social necessity for the piano duet has vanished. In addition another valuable use of the piano duet has disappeared with the twentieth-century invention of the radio and the phonograph; it is no longer necessary now for music lovers to turn to piano duet arrangements if they wish to become acquainted with the great symphonic and chamber music repertory. Also, unfortunately for the piano duet, the character of twentieth century music, with its exploration of entirely new areas such as electronic music on one hand, and the rigid complexity of the twelve-tone system on the other, has tended to veer away from the more easy going musical climate of the nineteenth century, in which the piano duet was best able to flourish and develop. That is not to say that there haven't been twentieth-century piano duets, and some very fine ones, but they are no longer in the mainstream of the musical tendency of the time.

For better or worse the piano duet is largely a nineteenth-century art. At the moment, perhaps, the nineteenth century may be a little out of fashion. But what a wonderful century it was. Perhaps when we are a little further away from it, it will begin to take on something of the aspect of a golden age—in art, in literature, and nowhere more than in music. And then once more the neglected masterpieces of the piano duet will be cherished among the treasures of music.

# The Piano Duet Style

THIS book might well have been entitled "Chamber Music for the Piano"—for it is the very essence of the piano-duet style that it is a form of chamber music, as opposed to the virtuoso style that flourishes so beautifully in the piano solo or in the two-piano literature. Certainly it is no accident that the greatest piano virtuoso of them all, Franz Liszt, with his love of pianism in every form, left next to nothing in the way of original piano duet music, although he did write an extended composition for two pianos as well as his two brilliant piano concertos. On the other hand, Franz Schubert, the most characteristic and voluminous composer of piano duets, never in his life wrote a piano concerto or a two-piano piece, and his piano music breathes the very spirit of an intimate chamber music style.

However, the opposition to a virtuoso style in the piano duet does not preclude an approach to an orchestral style, and it is a fascinating thing to observe how in certain cases the piano duet medium takes on something of the nature of an orchestral sketch without losing its own charm as a pianistic form. Schubert's "Grand Duo," for example, is so broad in conception and execution that some musicians, notably Schumann and Donald Francis Tovey, have been tempted to believe that it must be an arrangement of Schubert's lost "Gastein" Symphony. Yet it is in an unalloyed delight for two pianists to play together, and what could be a more perfect touchstone of the piano duet style in its delicacy and chamber music feeling than the following passage from the first movement:

The orchestral tendencies of the piano duet style have tempted many composers to orchestrate their own compositions for piano duet, and the piano duet form is so little practiced these days that these transcriptions have inevitably become more familiar than the originals, as in the case of Dvorak's "Slavonic Dances," for example, or Ravel's suite, "Ma mère l'oye." Indeed, the literature of the piano duet has provided numerous examples of transcriptions that have rescued the originals from oblivion. How many who know Schubert's "Marche Militaire" as an orchestral piece have ever heard it in its original form as a piano duet? Or of the innumerable organists who have played Schumann's lovely "Abendlied," how many suspect that it is from a set of twelve piano duets for children? Or for that matter, how many pianists know that Brahms' Waltzes were originally written for piano duet, and are much more grateful and idiomatic pianistically in that medium?

Of course arrangements have been made the other way too, and in the nineteenth century the custom of four-hand playing was so widespread that almost every major work, whether chamber music or orchestral, was likely to appear in a piano duet arrangement along with its version in the original form. Often the composers themselves made these arrangements, and in general a high level of taste and musicianship prevailed. They were a very convenient way of becoming acquainted with the masterworks of music in the days before radios and phonographs, and one need not dismiss them out of hand. Certainly they had, and even still have, a place from an educational point of view.

But the art of the piano duet is properly concerned with music that was conceived and composed for the medium. The literature is not very great compared with the riches of the piano solo literature. But there are some wonderful things in it that do not deserve to be lost.

III   **The Early Days**
         *J. C. Bach and Mozart*

ALTHOUGH the history of the piano duet can hardly be said to begin before the latter part of the eighteenth century, you may be interested as a matter of curiosity to look into the only two duet compositions still extant from the days of the harpsichord. Both are by English composers of the early seventeenth century, Nicholas Carlton and Thomas Tompkins; both are published together in a little album put out by Schott and Company; and fortunately both are charming pieces of considerably more than historic interest. Carlton is a minor composer of whom Grove can tell us hardly more than a few words, and of whom we have nothing in print besides this little duet piece. It is a charming thing nevertheless, a delicate web of contrapuntal tracery built around the plainsong chant, "In Nomine," and when played sensitively can recover for us much of the delicate musical flavor of its period.

Tompkins is a composer of greater importance whose keyboard and choral compositions have been extensively reprinted in England, and his mastery is clearly evident in this piece, which is developed on a broad scale and builds up at the end to a climax of great power. The notation of the Schott edition is somewhat misleading, for the editor has shortened the notes and introduced bar lines at regular intervals whereas the original manuscript is very freely barred. A comparison of the opening of the primo part in both versions will show what a different musical impression is created by the altered notation:

Original      I

Schott Edition   I

Don't be misled by the steady two-beat barring of the new version into an interpretation at variance with the character of the piece. It is not *allegro energico* but rather *andantino un poco sostenuto,* and although there are no markings of any kind, you can imagine the subtle shadings of a vocal choir. At the same time it is clearly an instrumental piece, written antiphonally for the two players, and as the massed thirds increase in strength and intensity toward the end, you can allow yourself a certain freedom in performance. It would be hard to avoid increasing the tempo a little as the piece gathers momentum, and certainly the character of the music suggests a powerful crescendo at the last page.

How completely these two beautiful pieces had been forgotten in the next century can be inferred from the fact that when the celebrated musical historian Charles Burney presented a duet sonata to the public in 1777 he felt obliged to justify the novelty of this strange medium in the following charming *apologia:*

> As the following sonata is the first that has appeared in print of its kind it may be necessary to say something concerning its utility. That great and varied effects may be produced by duets on two keyboards has been proved by several ingenious compositions, some of which have been published in Germany. But the inconvenience of having two harpsichords or pianofortes in the same room has prevented the cultivation of this species of music. The playing of duets by two performers upon one instrument is, however, attended with nearly as many advantages without the inconvenience of crowding a room, and although at first the near approach of the hands of the

different players may seem awkward or embarrassing, a little use and contrivance with respect to the manner of placing them, and the choice of fingers, will soon remove that difficulty.

One of Burney's piano duet sonatas has been included in a fascinating anthology of early duet music put out by the Theodore Presser Company, and edited by that excellent and indefatigable scholar, Douglas Townsend.* It must be confessed that Burney's sonata is of primarily historic interest, for it is in fact rather featureless and rambling, and suggests nothing so much as a kind of watered down C. P. E. Bach. But this collection is well worth having, not only for the antiquarian interest of Burney's sonata, and a few others by minor composers of the period, but because it contains a few splendid pieces by Haydn and Clementi that may be not be easily accessible elsewhere.

For practical purposes, however, the history of the piano duet begins with Johann Christian Bach, the youngest son of the great Sebastian, who settled in England and is remembered as the London Bach. J. C. Bach is the first incontrovertible master to leave a considerable body of work for the piano duet, and three admirable sonatas of his are still in print in the Peters Edition.

Mozart in his letters refers to J. C. Bach as a great composer, and we need look no further than these three sonatas for the evidence of it. They are broad in scope, masterly in execution, and filled with delightful and original touches. The style strikes us now as Mozartean, but it is Mozartean only in that Mozart founded his style so largely on J. C. Bach. It takes a little acquaintance with Bach's style to recognize how his idiom differs from Mozart's, for at first sight they are almost indistinguishable. Bach is more controlled and though not lacking in passion, shows a certain sense of restraint. Mozart is freer and more varied in phrasing and invention. Bach leads us through formal gardens; Mozart through a landscape often touched with magic. Bach is of his time; Mozart is timeless.

It is the tragedy of J. C. Bach, as it was of Buxtehude before him, that he developed an entirely personal and distinctive style that we can no longer recognize as his own because another and greater com-

---

* *Piano Duets of the Classical Period;* Theodore Presser Co., Bryn Mawr, Pa.

poser has developed and transcended it. But J. C. Bach, like Buxtehude, is still well worth knowing in his own right; after a while we can recognize his own tone of voice, and there will be some days when we wish for his company and no one else's.

Here is an excerpt from the rondo of J. C. Bach's sonata in C, which offers a good idea of his style, and which when compared with the rondo theme of Mozart's C major sonata shows something of the nature of Mozart's indebtedness to him.

J. C. Bach

The three sonatas of J. C. Bach in the Peters Edition were originally published in 1778 and 1780, and although some of his unpublished

four-hand pieces are earlier in date, it is curious that Mozart's earliest essays in the form of the piano duet actually antedate J. C. Bach's. In 1765, when the nine-year-old Mozart and his sister were visiting London, Leopold Mozart wrote to a friend at home: ". . . little Wolfgang has composed his first sonata for four hands; up till now no four-hand sonata has been composed anywhere." Christian Bach may well have been acquainted with this sonata, for he was friendly with little Wolfgang during his fourteen-month stay in London, in spite of being twenty-one years his senior. Indeed, the friendship between Mozart and J. C. Bach, entirely free of either envy or condescension, is one of the heartwarming personal events in musical history.

This sonata of Mozart's boyhood has had a curious history. The manuscript was lost, and when the eighteenth-century editions of the work disappeared, the sonata dropped out of sight entirely. It was not until 1921 that the great Mozart scholar St-Foix ran across a copy that had lain in the archives of the *Bibliothèque Nationale* in Paris, and later the English musicologist A. Hyatt King discovered an English edition, which the Oxford University Press reprinted in 1952.

The work is an amazing one for a nine-year-old boy, and along with the *First Symphony* in E flat, K. 16, also dating from the same London visit, represents a high water mark in the child Mozart's output at this time. It is in three movements, an allegro, a minuet and trio, and a final rondo, each fairly extended for this phase of Mozart's development. Here and there it is possible to find occasional traces of awkwardness or naiveté in the harmony or construction, which we can't help cherishing, for we shall never find them again in Mozart.

The sonata as a whole is wonderfully fresh and inventive, and from the first Mozart shows a perfect mastery of his instrumental medium. This work could not be mistaken for a symphony, or indeed for anything but a piano duet. Witness the opening of the second theme:

In the recapitulation the players reverse the roles, the upper taking the scales, and the lower the melody.

Mozart was to make the piano duet medium very much his own, and of the other four completed sonatas that he left, the last two in F and C which show him at the height of his powers, are landmarks in the history of the medium. The earlier two are delightful in their own way, but are smaller in scale—somewhat smaller than J. C. Bach's sonatas, for example—and the finales of both, though brilliant, are a trifle perfunctory.

Charles Burney, in his *Musical Voyage Through Germany and The Netherlands,* published in 1773, mentions that one of his correspondents visited the Mozart family in Salzburg in 1772 and found Wolfgang and his sister playing duets. Very likely the visitor may have heard Mozart's next sonata in D, K.381 (123a), which dates from that year when Mozart was sixteen. What a delightful, alert and inventive work it is. Mozart was a full-fledged master by then, and the work is boyish only in its high spirits and cheerfulness. There is an unusual experiment in sonority in the slow movement, where the melody of the second theme is doubled at a distance of two octaves:

Can this be the source of that most characteristically Mozartean touch of orchestral wizardry, the doubling of the flute and bassoon two octaves apart, as in the overture to the *Magic Flute* and the finale of the G minor symphony?

The next sonata in B flat, K.358 (186c), which dates from Mozart's eighteenth year, is very similar in general mood, bright, good humored and to the point. This sonata too has a lovely slow movement which is the high point of the work.

With the next sonata in F, K.497, we come to the great Mozart. Composed in 1786, the year after *Figaro,* this work is conceived on as broad a scale as anything Mozart ever wrote, and it ranks with the greatest of his chamber music works. Tovey has included a study of it in the first volume of his *Essays in Musical Analysis,* and in case you don't know Tovey yet, it's time you did, so look him up. As always, his depth of musical understanding and poetical intuition are beyond praise.

This sonata begins with a slow introduction, always something of a rarity in Mozart. As in the few other cases where he introduces one, such as the great E flat major symphony and the quintet for piano and winds, he almost seems to be saying: "I am in a serious mood today, so prepare yourself for something particularly fine!" This movement must have made a great impression on the young Beethoven, for there is more than one echo of it in his early work, and in retrospect, it almost seems to take on something of the character of Beethoven's first period style. Here is how the introduction begins:

There is a suggestion in these bars of the introduction to Beethoven's *First Symphony,* but while Beethoven's introduction is over almost before it has begun, Mozart's continues through some very beautiful modulations before at last reaching the opening theme of the *Allegro di molto:*

Tovey has confessed to a secret desire to transcribe this sonata for string quintet, and the alternation between the registers of the two pianists does call to mind one of Mozart's favorite devices in his quintet writing, the alternation of the higher and lower strings, with the viola first acting as the bass to the two violins, and then taking the melody above the lower strings.

Often it is helpful and stimulating at the piano to imagine the tone color of orchestral instruments, and in this case you can equally well imagine the cooler tone of the orchestral winds, say the flutes and clarinets alternating with the horns and bassoons; the violins then entering at the eighth-note passages in the upper part, the full orchestra at the forte passage and the strings alone at the little transition theme which follows. Indeed, it would be tempting to transcribe the entire work for small orchestra, except that at some point or other we would feel impelled to introduce the piano—so perhaps we may as well leave it in Mozart's original form after all and enjoy it as a piano duet. The first movement is in Mozart's best vein throughout, with a finely conceived development section, and an amusing and witty coda.

The second movement is one of Mozart's gravest and most serenely peaceful slow movements. The finale is again Mozart at the top of his form, a spacious and highly organized rondo based on this engaging melody:

There is not room to quote as fully as we might like from this rondo but here at least is a little transition theme, which Mozart casts in a new light every time it returns. This is its first appearance:

And here is its metamorphosis in the coda:

The next and last of Mozart's piano duet sonatas, in C, K.521, was written in the following year, and is a worthy companion to this one. Although lighter in style, as evinced for example in the easy-going development section of the first movement (which as so often with Mozart in his lighter moods, is not really a development at all), it is still adorable Mozart all the way through. Somewhat more brilliant pianistically than the F major sonata, it approaches a little Mozart's concerto style, and when Mozart sent it off to his friend Jacquin to give to his sister, he wrote: "Tell her to start practicing immediately, for it is the very devil to play!" Keep the tempo fast, by the way, when you perform this piece, for this movement must be light and brisk if it is to get off the ground.

The slow movement is charming, and its middle section, a romantic episode in D minor, strikes the deepest note in the work. The finale, whose theme we quoted earlier in the chapter, is Mozart in a relaxed and good-humored vein. This rondo presents no musical problems, although perhaps a few technical ones.

Mozart's only other sonata for piano duet is, like the early sonata in C, something of a special case, and is not included in most editions of the Mozart piano duets. It dates from 1786, and Mozart completed the first movement only till bar 99, a few bars past the exposition, and the slow movement till bar 159 at the end of the first episode in C. For many years it remained a tantalizing fragment, like so many others of Mozart's unfinished sketches that look out at us from the pages of the Köchel thematic catalogue, seeming to be almost more pregnant with possibilities than many of the completed works. In 1853 the two movements were completed by Julius André, the son of the publisher Johann André, who had originally received this sonata from Mozart's sister. In the first movement André has extended the development section slightly, cleverly utilizing Mozart's material, and constructed a recapitulation where nothing is changed except for the necessary alternation of key. In the second movement André has contented himself with a brief coda based on Mozart's opening section. André has performed his task of reconstruction with skill and tact, and in its present form has given us a Mozart sonata that we can be very grateful for.

The first movement begins with this bold theme in octaves:

It continues in terse and energetic style, moving to the dominant without even pausing for any clearly defined "second theme." At the first cadence in the dominant, Mozart takes us by surprise with this unexpected modulation:

The second movement is sketchier than the first, but it does contain a few pleasant moments, such as this charming anticipation of Schubert's "Viennese" style:

In the same key and dating from the same year is one of Mozart's loveliest and most perfect shorter works, a set of variations on an original theme, K. 501. Alfred Einstein in his masterly study of Mozart suggests that it may have been conceived as a part of the above sonata, and whether or not this is the case, it must have stemmed from the same period of preoccupation with the piano duet.

If Mozart ever identified his pieces as musical portraits of his friends, as Schumann and Elgar were later to do, then this might well have been the portrait of a gracious and lovely girl of, say, fifteen. The theme has an almost articulate character as though she were, perhaps, welcoming friends who had dropped by. In the first variation she might be discussing casual matters, while in the second she seems to be bustling about some household chores. In the third we surprise her up to mischief, while in the fourth she turns into a perfect angel. The finale brings us back to earth again, and ends with a last glimpse of the theme in its original form. If there were anyone who knew no Mozart at all, this piece would be an excellent introduction to his music, for it is as "Mozartean" as anything he ever wrote.

The list of Mozart's music for piano duet is completed with a fugue in G minor, K. 401, of which the last eight bars were completed by the Abbé Stadler. Actually this work is hardly a piece for the piano duet, since there is nothing at all pianistic about it. It is as though Mozart wished to try his hand at a fugue, and found it easier to do for piano duet than for piano solo, not wishing to limit himself to the range and capacity of two hands. There is another fugue of Mozart's C minor for two pianos, which Mozart later arranged for string quartet and provided with a beautiful adagio for an introduction. If

Johann Christian Bach (oil painting by Gainsborough).

Mozart had done the same for this piece, no doubt we should know it better, for it is well worth a hearing.

Although this completes the list of Mozart's four-hand music, there are two other pieces that deserve mention here; the two fantasies in F minor, K. 594 and K. 608, for they are best known in their duet version although originally composed for "an organ in a clock." The instrument for which these two compositions were commissioned was a mechanical organ of limited range and capabilities, and Mozart began his task with some impatience at the limitations of the instrument. He writes to his wife on October 3, 1790:

> I have now made up my mind to compose at once the adagio for my watchmaker and then to slip a few ducats into the hand of my dear little wife. And this I have done; but as it is a kind of composition which I detest, I have unfortunately not been able to finish it. I compose a bit of it every day—but I have to break off now and then as I get bored. And indeed I would give the whole thing up, if I had not such an important reason to go on with it. But I still hope that I shall gradually be able to force myself to finish it. If it were for a large instrument and the work would sound like an organ piece, then I might get some fun out of it. But, as it is, the works consist solely of little pipes, which sound too high pitched and childish for my taste.

But curiously enough, Mozart's irritation does not seem to have affected the quality of his inspiration. The first of the two works, K. 594, begins with a beautiful adagio which must have sounded exquisite on the high-pitched instrument for which it was originally written. The allegro which follows is in a kind of Handelian contrapuntal style, and a return to the opening adagio brings the composition to a close.

By the time Mozart got around to the second of the fantasies, K. 608, he had attained the full flight of his inspiration. Here he actually created a contrapuntal and fugal form of his own, incorporating elements of the sonata and the prelude and fugue, as well as the old toccata form in which an early fugal section returns in a varied form later in the composition. This is one of Mozart's greatest works, and in its version as an organ piece it represents one of the high points of the organ literature.

But these two pieces for mechanical organ were actually written by Mozart on four staves, which may have suggested to Mozart's early publishers the possibility for their use as piano duets, and they first appeared in print arranged for piano duet. It was in this form that Schubert became acquainted with them, and the influence they had on Schubert can be seen in a number of his compositions, most particularly in the great fantasy in F minor for four hands, opus 103, in which the imprint of the second of Mozart's fantasies is unmistakable.

Among Mozart's younger contemporaries who experimented with the duet form, one of the most talented was Dussek, who played a great part in the musical life of his time, and whose influence extended over many decades. Mendelssohn has called Dussek "a prodigal," and a glance at his compositions will reveal the acuteness of this remark; they are filled with brilliant ideas in plenty, and fall short of the highest level chiefly in Dussek's lack of inclination to develop and refine them to the fullest degree. Sometimes they remind one of the earlier sketches for Beethoven's compositions; the ideas are there, and the style and the character, but we feel that they fall short of their final stage of perfection. All the same, Dussek's piano sonatas have proved worthy of revival, and Eric Blom has written an interesting essay analyzing the whole series of them, thirty-two in all (the same number as Beethoven's) dating from before 1790 to 1811. They have been republished in Czechoslovakia as a national undertaking, for Dussek was a Czech, one of the earliest in a line of masters that culminated a century later in Dvorak and Smetana.

Dussek was almost as exclusively a piano composer as Chopin, and the complete list of his works includes very little not written for that instrument. Dussek's duet sonatas are very numerous, sixteen in all according to the catalogue in Grove, and it is very much to be hoped that they will be reprinted as a series, for on the basis of what we already know of Dussek there is no doubt that there will be many fine things among them. One of Dussek's duet sonatas, the second, opus 48 in C, was put out by the firm of Heugel in Paris in the last century, and although it is now out of print, an examination of it at the Library of Congress shows it to be a splendid work, brilliant and virtuoso in style, with a fine and imaginative slow movement.

Three duet sonatinas reprinted recently by the firm of Elkan-Vogel

are well worth having. They are his opus 67, which Dussek has entitled "Sonatas progressives," and which are obviously intended as
educational material, for in them Dussek nowhere approaches anything like the brilliant and quite difficult pianistic style of his opus 48.
But they are charming and excellent teaching pieces for students on
an intermediate level. Eric Blom has entitled his essay on Dussek
"The Prophecies of Dussek," for he has discovered striking anticipa-
tions of Schubert, Liszt, Brahms and even Richard Strauss. Is it perhaps not too fanciful to imagine that in such a theme as this from the
second of the three sonatinas, there is something of the Bohemian
quality of Dvorak that we find in certain of the Slavonic Dances?

Equally a master, although in a very different way, is Muzio Clementi. His music is clearer and more consistent than Dussek's, but
still has spirit and style. In one of Mozart's letters there is a rather
slighting reference to Clementi, with whom Mozart once had a friendly
passage at arms at improvising. But as a number of annotators have
pointed out, this comment was made before Clementi had reached his
full maturity as a composer. Beethoven had the highest opinion of
him, and so did every musician, great or small, up to the time of
Brahms and later. Clementi's magnum opus is his series of exercises,
"Gradus ad Parnassum," which was daily bread to generations of
master pianists, and which is still worth knowing. In addition Clementi had a particular genius for writing interesting and skillful compositions on a level that beginning pianists can handle, and he has
achieved a kind of immortality in this genre.

For piano duet Clementi has written seven sonatas, which are all
still in print. They are excellent, beautifully written for the instrument, and imaginatively conceived in terms of the two pianists. This
excerpt from the sonata in E flat, opus 16 number 1, will give you some
idea of his style:

In his own day, Pleyel was as highly esteemed as Clementi or Dussek, and at the beginning of his career Mozart expressed the hope that he might someday fill the shoes of his teacher Haydn. But although technically expert, Pleyel's works are lacking in strength and fire. Two of his duet sonatas have been reprinted, and you may wish to look them up as representative examples of the style of his day.

But what about Haydn himself? Well, Haydn wasn't particularly interested in the piano duet. In the complete catalogue of his voluminous output by Anthony van Hoboken, there are only two listings for piano duet, both early works and both trifles. The set of variations entitled "Master and Scholar" is the better known of the two; it has been reprinted many times, and indeed it is a most useful piece for any teacher and pupil to work at together. The lower pianist, the teacher, starts each phrase by himself, as though to show how it should be done, the higher pianist, the pupil, repeats it exactly two octaves higher, and then each section is finished with both teacher and pupil playing together for a few bars. There are seven variations, each following exactly the same pattern, with the figuration becoming progressively more difficult at each new variation. Not very important Haydn, perhaps, but a clever and amusing *pièce d'occasion.*

The other Haydn duet, a partita in two movements, existed for a long time only in an undated manuscript copy and was entirely neglected until its publication recently in Douglas Townsend's collection and in a Schirmer anthology. The first movement begins as though it might be a finger exercise by almost any anonymous composer of the period, but as it goes on it acquires a drive and spirit that no anonymous composer of the period could have attained. The minuet and trio that follows is obviously an early work, and has a little of the stiffness of the early quartets. But before it is over we can catch Haydn smiling from behind his old-fashioned peruke; he is the same good fellow as always and there is no resisting him.

# IV   *Beethoven*

For MOST of us, Beethoven stands at the center of the musical universe. In almost every field he touched, the symphony, the string quartet, the sonata for piano, violin or cello, his contribution has become the major bulwark of the repertory. However, like Haydn, he does not seem to have been particularly interested in the piano duet; perhaps he was too much of an individualist, too much of a virtuoso, to wish to share his instrument with a partner, and in this book the center of gravity has shifted ahead a little to Schubert. But all the same, every one of Beethoven's piano duet works is important, and every note of them is important. Schumann once remarked that even a chromatic scale by Beethoven is different from anyone else's, and somehow there is a peculiar intensity about Beethoven's music that you cannot escape.

Beethoven's output for the piano duet comprises an early sonata and two early sets of variations, a fascinating set of three marches that dates from the period of the *Eroica* symphony, and one work of his last period, his own piano duet arrangement of the "Grosse Fugue."

The little piano duet sonata in D, opus 6, is among the shortest and slightest of all the sonatas that Beethoven published himself (for of course the two sonatinas of opus 49 were published without his knowledge or permission), and its two movements seem almost to hark back to the two-movement form of J. C. Bach. Yet at the same time it looks ahead—not actually to the two-movement form of the sonatas of Beethoven's last period, for they are too distant in style and content—but rather to such a two-movement sonata of Beethoven's middle period as opus 54; or perhaps even more to the little three-movement sonata, opus 79, which like it, seems at first glance to be rather slight, but which reveals more than you expect when you study it more deeply.

The first movement of this duet sonata should not be taken too slowly or too lightly; the *allegro molto* direction is very important, and it must be played in a strongly masculine manner, particularly in the terse development section and at the unexpected appearance of the minor mode during the recapitulation. The second theme is in a more gracious mood, as this brief excerpt will show:

Do not slow it down, however, or yield to the temptation of sentimentality—rather emphasize its humorous aspect in the *sforzando* third beat of the accompaniment. The rondo finale is more luxuriant and flowing; here you may allow it something of the character of a slow movement, without however taking it too slowly. Perhaps the tempo of a leisurely minuet might be closest in feeling to the style of this piece, if you can imagine a minuet in 4/4 time.

The appearance of the minor mode in the first episode lends the piece, as in the corresponding section of the first movement, a new dimension of strength. But the second episode, a dialogue between the two players, is in a lighter and more playful mood. Slight as this work is, Beethoven knew perfectly well what he was doing in acknowledging its paternity, for it is worthy of him.

In the variation form as in the sonata form Beethoven is the supreme master, and the two volumes of his variations for solo piano tower over the rest of the variation literature as his sonatas tower over the rest of the sonata literature. The larger bulk of his variations date from his earlier years, when he was learning and developing his craft through the use of this form. Numerous as they are, it is remarkable how each one of them is a completely independent and unique entity, as different from one another as each of the sonatas.

Both of Beethoven's sets of variations for four hands date from his earlier years, and both are delightful and characteristic examples of his treatment of the form. Neither has an opus number, but the earlier of the two, dating from 1791, is the set of variations in C on this charming theme of Count Waldstein:

Certainly Beethoven was fortunate to have lived in a circle where even patrons of music could compose a theme like this. Notice how cleverly it is constructed, alternating phrases of six and four bars as well as the major and minor modes. Beethoven's variations are admirably resourceful and contrasted; there is a brilliant pianistic climax in the sixth variation, and a lovely eighth variation in the minor, after which Beethoven breaks off into a freer and more improvisatory section to finish the work, humorously alternating passages between the players in *adagio* and *presto* tempo.

The variations in D, on an original theme of Beethoven's to words of Goethe, first took shape in 1799 in the musical album of the sisters Josephine and Theresa von Brunswick. Beethoven thought well enough of the piece to extend it for publication a few years later by adding two new variations, now the fourth and fifth of the set. Originally a slight but charming *pièce d'occasion,* it is interesting to observe how Beethoven gave the work new depth with the two additional variations. Here is the beginning of the fourth variation, which clearly belongs to a more mature period of Beethoven's development than the preceding variations.

As with the variations in C on the theme of his friend and patron, Count Waldstein, the personal associations of this work lend it a special interest, for Beethoven is known to have been romantically involved with both the Brunswick sisters.

In a different vein are the three marches of opus 45, formidably powerful pieces that put one in mind of Beethoven's remark that if he were a soldier he could have taught Napoleon a lesson. Playing these marches, etched in iron, as it were, one is quite ready to believe him. Although they are masterfully written for the piano, they contain passages that suggest orchestral color, and it is not surprising that a number of musicians have given them new settings for band or for orchestra. Listen to the trio of the second march, for example, where you can almost hear the drums in the bass and the fifes in the treble:

These marches are Beethoven at his best, and they may very likely have given Schubert the cue for his own numerous series of piano duet marches.

With the "Grosse Fuge," we are again in a different world. This work is something of a special case in Beethoven's duet music in that it is a transcription of a work originally conceived for another medium. But it is well to remember that Beethoven, like Bach and Mozart, had no particular inhibitions about transcribing his own music for other instrumental combinations, and while his transcriptions are not too numerous, they all possess features of exceptional interest. Particularly instructive is the string quartet arrangement of his early piano sonata, opus 14 no. 1, which he wrote specially to demonstrate the freedom that must be taken in adapting a work for another medium. The piano concerto version of the violin concerto is another interesting example; although this is perhaps less of an artistic than a practical undertaking, since it was written largely at the insistence of his publisher, Clementi, who wished to capitalize on Beethoven's celebrity as a piano composer.

Certainly one of the most fascinating of Beethoven's own transcriptions is the version he made of his "Grosse Fuge" for string quartet, opus 133, for piano duet as opus 134. The "Grosse Fuge," it will be remembered, was originally the last movement of the great B flat string quartet, opus 130, but when the work proved to be excessively long in its original form, Beethoven allowed himself to be persuaded that a short and lively finale would be a more appropriate ending to the quartet, and agreed to publish the fugue as a separate composition. As such, it is, along with the fugue of the "Hammerclavier" sonata, one of the most remarkable of Beethoven's last period experiments in fugal form. But since it is extremely difficult for string quartet, and since string quartet groups would in any case be unlikely to perform such an unwieldy and anomalous work by itself, Beethoven's publisher, Artaria, felt the desirability of offering it in a more accessible medium. The piano of course would have been an obvious answer, but as no single pianist could have possibly handled the work, the piano duet must have suggested itself as a more practical alternative.* It must be admitted that in its piano duet version the work has not really made its way, no doubt because of its extreme musical as well as pianistic difficulty. All the same, it is a fascinating work and should be known and studied much more widely than it is.

* The work was first given to Anton Halm to transcribe, but Beethoven was dissatisfied with the result and took it in hand himself.

Beethoven has handled the transcription with considerable freedom in his effort to make the work more pianistic, sometimes altering a contrapuntal line in order to facilitate the crossing of the hands, sometimes changing repeated notes into a tremolo pattern, and often extending the bass line below the range of the cello. Incidentally, conductors who are interested in performing the work for string orchestra would be well advised to study the piano duet version very carefully in this respect, for Beethoven has varied the bass line with the greatest possible sensitivity and imagination. Notice bars 56 to 58, for example, where the bass line is brought down an octave and then doubled at the lower octave, while the tenor part in turn is taken down to the lower octave. But in spite of Beethoven's best intentions, it must be confessed that the work is not really pianistic, and it is hardly possible to think of it in terms of actual performance. But as an opportunity to learn and study one of Beethoven's most extraordinary compositions, it is invaluable.

If you really want to explore this piece, you had better prepare yourself by a very serious effort at analyzing it before you start. Number the measures from beginning to end,* mark the entrances and the variations of the subject and countersubjects, and study its form, both in regard to the fugal rules and in regard to Beethoven's great freedom in handling them. Chart out a map of the territory first and know its geography very well before you venture into it; otherwise you are likely to get caught up in the maze of detail, and may easily lose track of the larger contours of this wonderful territory.

Notice first that the fugue proper starts at the end of bar 33; the opening section is marked by Beethoven as the "Overtura" and is devoted chiefly to outlining the main theme of the composition, a powerful chromatic motive which pervades the entire composition from beginning to end:

---

* Note that there is an extra measure in the duet version from the very beginning, for Beethoven has extended the opening quartet fermata by one bar in making it into a tremolo.

You will notice that this does not become the fugue subject itself, but appears as a countersubject when the subject makes its appearance with this bold and leaping theme:

Beethoven has notated this countersubject in the rather strange form of two tied eighth notes, which may possibly suggest a certain kind of interpretive finesse to a string player, but which a pianist has no way of bringing out. Yet Beethoven has not altered it in the piano version; if he had, the result would have appeared as follows:

which somehow seems inexpressibly crude after the string version. Even though you can do nothing with this figure at the piano, think of it as two eighth notes all the same; perhaps it may have a certain psychological value in helping you to feel the piece as Beethoven did.

Note as some of the main events in the development of the fugue proper the appearance of a new triplet countersubject at bar 66, and the introduction of a new rhythm of an eighth and two sixteenths at bar 112. At bar 140 the countersubject moves twice as fast by eliminating the quarter-note rest, as the subject appears in a new triplet diminution. The tension has been mounting all this time, but at bar 161 Beethoven introduces a slower section, *meno mosso e moderato,* which provides an interlude of peace and benediction. This passage is based entirely on the motive of the opening, and as you play it strive for the kind of tranquillity that the string tone can offer. In the original version, Beethoven has made use a little later on in this section of repeated sixteenth notes, which can be played in a quiet and almost soothing manner by the strings, but in the duet version Beethoven has sensitively transformed them into a new pianistic equivalent:

Now we plunge headlong into the last and longest section of the work (*allegro* in the duet version, but *allegro molto e con brio* in the quartet version), as the material based almost entirely on the opening motive in strangely varied guises, seems to hurry on desperately to a tragic end. There are passages of brief respite, as in the momentary reintroduction of the *meno mosso* section; or, at bar 613, this strangely spiritual version of the motive:

But nothing can serve to halt the mounting tension and excitement of this powerful work as it heads on at an ever-accelerated rate to a breathless close. It is a strange and difficult piece of intense nervous energy and intellectual concentration, but one that you must know if you wish to understand Beethoven, and to glimpse the extraordinary development that took place in his style in his last years. If Beethoven had only lived a little longer, certainly he would have developed and revolutionized the fugal form as completely as he did the sonata and the variation form.

Among the composers who lived and worked in Beethoven's orbit, his pupil Karl Czerny was no doubt the most brilliant pianist. We remember Czerny today as the author of innumerable technical exercises which are at once both clever and practical, but Czerny also composed more serious and ambitious things, and Horowitz among other pianists has occasionally brought one or another of them to the concert platform. Czerny shared the general interest of his period in the piano duet, and has left a number of works in this medium, one of which has been recently reprinted by Douglas Townsend, a charming and well-written sonatina that is most useful for students. Czerny even experimented with the novel idea of a concerto for piano duet and orchestra, but since the piano duet style is basically inimical to the concerto style which demands virtuosity rather than intimacy, this work has remained something of a curiosity, rather like Spohr's concerto for string quartet and orchestra which has similarly mismated the intimate string-quartet style with the virtuoso character of the concerto. All the same it is a masterly work, conceived on broad architectural lines, which suggests that Czerny has been considerably underestimated as a serious composer.

Interesting too are Czerny's pioneering experiments in writing for six hands at one piano, which include a set of six excellent and somewhat extended pieces published under the general title of "Les Pianistes Associés." Czerny has handled this novel medium very cleverly, giving each of the players his own chance to shine, and making the very most of the opportunities for virtuosity in this extremely limited medium. Although it is not easy to be serious about the thought of three players crowded together at one piano, it is tempting to imagine what three virtuosi—let us say Horowitz, Rubinstein and Serkin—might do with these pieces in a light-hearted mood.

Like Czerny, Ferdinand Ries was one of Beethoven's pupils, and if he is remembered now purely for his association with Beethoven, he was still a composer of great influence in his day who wrote voluminously for piano duet. One of his piano duet compositions, a set of variations on a national air of Thomas Moore, is interesting not only for its own sake, but as the direct inspiration for Chopin's only duet composition, an early set of variations on another of Moore's national airs.

To most of us nowadays the name Diabelli serves only to identify Beethoven's greatest set of variations. But actually Anton Diabelli was a sympathetic personality in his own right, who lived at the very center of the musical life of Vienna during its golden age as one of its leading publishers. Diabelli was a gifted composer as well, who survives to this day by virtue of a very clever series of duets that he wrote for teaching purposes. They are based on the idea of limiting the upper part to a range of five notes, played in octaves with each hand in an unchanging position so that it can be played by pupils from the very earliest days of their musical study. Diabelli has handled this idea with great skill and charm, and the best of his compositions of this type are still in print in almost every country of the world, and still continue to give pleasure to student and teacher alike. This idea has proved so fruitful for educational purposes that a number of later composers have copied it in their own way, among them, to name but a few, Carl Reinecke, César Cui, Florent Schmitt, André Caplet and Leopold Godowsky.

Speaking of piano duets for educational purposes, we should not forget the name of Friedrich Kuhlau whose excellent sonatinas for piano solo are still found in many anthologies. Kuhlau also left a number of similar sonatinas for piano duet, which although less familiar are still most valuable for teaching purposes, and which are fortunately still in print as published by Peters.

By all contemporary accounts, the one composer of Beethoven's time who came nearest to being regarded as his equal was Mozart's favorite pupil, Hummel, and indeed Jan Nepomuk Hummel was a composer of unusual gifts. A few of his compositions, notably his piano concertos in A minor and B minor have found a new lease on life through the medium of long-playing records, and have proved to have a considerable appeal to listeners of our own day. Hummel's style is smoother than Beethoven's, and it must be confessed, much more innocuous, but he excels him perhaps, in the ease and polish of his piano writing, which had a great influence on the piano style of such greater composers as Chopin and Liszt. Actually in his own day, it seemed perfectly natural for his contemporaries to place him on equal terms with the greatest, and this excerpt from a letter of Liszt, written in the 1830's, is quite typical:

> My mind and my fingers are working like two lost souls. . . . Beethoven, Bach, Hummel, Mozart, Weber are all about me. I study them, meditate on them, devour them furiously.

Hummel has left two sonatas for piano duet, opus 51 in E flat and opus 92 in A flat, of which the latter is the more serious and ambitious work. Its first two movements are very fine, and this excerpt from the first movement will suggest something of the individual quality of virtuosity that Hummel brought to the duet medium:

The finale, however, is weaker, and rambles on at length in a pleasant and inconsequential way. Somehow Schubert's rambling finales seem to be illuminated by the genius of his earlier movements, but Hummel's first two movements are not quite strong enough to carry this finale, and the total effect is weakened by it. Among Hummel's other duet works is a Notturno, opus 91, which also exists in a version with two obbligato horns, a set of pleasant variations on a folk-like tune, preceded by a solemn and rather pompous introduction in the minor.

Hummel has also written a set of waltzes for piano duet, opus 99, followed by, of all things, a musical representation of a battle, all in the same steady waltz tempo. These waltzes are tuneful and bucolic in a most agreeable way, and call to mind the ease and gaiety of Mozart's Viennese dances. The third is entitled "La Chasse," the fifth "Alla Turca," while the sixth leads directly into the battle, complete with imitations of trumpets and drums, a quotation of "Marlborough," and a section entitled "La Victoire" ending with a final fugato and coda. Beethoven once wrote a pot-boiler for orchestra entitled the *Battle Symphony,* but it is hard to imagine him capable of the sublime irrelevance of a battle in waltz time. And yet this series of *valses, suivis d'une bataille* might well prove the most performable of Hummel's duet works, if you can only contrive to view it as a period piece of curiosity and charm.

# V    Schubert

## The Variations
## and Divertissements

SCHUBERT is perhaps something of a special case among the composers. Certainly his place in the pantheon of the great masters is assured—yet there is a delicacy and intimacy about his style that some listeners are impervious to. With him, more than most other composers, there is the likelihood that you may either adore him or be indifferent to him. Even so acute a critic as Debussy could ask when his *Unfinished Symphony* would ever be finished, and Wagner was always a little condescending about his Viennese strain. Yet Liszt and Brahms, two musicians as dissimilar as any who ever lived, were united in a fanatical devotion to Schubert. Liszt's well-known remark may well stand as the key to his magic and to his greatness: *Il était le musicien le plus poète qui fut jamais*—he was the most poetic musician who ever lived.

For those who love Schubert there is a largely undiscovered treasure in the vast body of music he left for piano duet. Uneven it certainly is, containing some of his finest and most characteristic work, as well as occasional pages that are trivial or uninspired. But as a whole, the level is remarkably high, and there is nothing that a Schubertian would willingly part with.

Often Schubert seems more comfortable in the medium of the piano duet than when writing for piano solo. As a pianist his conceptions sometimes exceed his technical grasp, and in much of his piano writing, the sonatas particularly, there is a certain sense of sketchiness in the execution. Not that they can't be given with powerful effect by an able and sympathetic pianist, but there is always an element of challenge and hazard, pianistically speaking. In the medium of the piano duet, however, his problems vanish, and he moves at his ease in an area where he is complete master.

The piano-duet form occupied Schubert for his entire career, from the earliest compositions of his childhood to the last year of his life. A goodly portion of Schubert's four-hand music dates from two extended visits to the summer home of Count Esterhazy in Zselis, Hungary, where he was music teacher to the count's two daughters. The entire family was gifted musically, and he was encouraged there to write much of his finest four-hand music.

The visits were six years apart, the first dating from 1818 when he was barely out of his teens. He had already written some of his finest songs, although none of the instrumental music by which we remember him, unless we except the early symphonies. The second visit was in 1824, when he already had the *Unfinished Symphony* and the "Wanderer Fantasy" behind him. During each of the two visits he wrote a sonata and a set of variations for piano duet as well as a host of smaller things.

Let us start with Schubert's first published work for piano duet, the "Variations on a French Air," opus 10, written during the first summer at Zselis. This work has the added interest of being one of the few links that connect Schubert and Beethoven during their lifetime. It was actually Schubert's first published instrumental work of any importance, his first nine opus numbers being songs and waltzes, and Schubert in his eagerness to pay homage to the giant who was his neighbor in Vienna immediately dedicated the work to him "from his worshipper and admirer, Franz Schubert."

Although it is certain that Beethoven knew the work and had a favorable opinion of Schubert through it, accounts differ as to its presentation to him. According to Schubert's and Beethoven's mutual friend, the composer Anselm Hüttenbrenner, Schubert brought it to Beethoven's lodgings and finding him out left it with a servant. Beethoven's biographer, Schindler, who was also acquainted with Schubert, has this account of it:

. . . . Schubert had an unhappy experience when, in 1822, he presented to the master a copy of his Variations for four hands which he had dedicated to him. The shy and speechless young composer contributed to his own embarrassment, in spite of the fact that he was introduced by Diabelli, who interpreted for him his feelings for the great man. The courage which had sustained him as far as the house forsook him completely in the presence of the prince of composers. . . . Beethoven ran through the variations and discovered a harmonic inaccuracy. He gently drew the young man's attention to this, adding that it was no deadly sin. But Schubert, perhaps as a result of this encouraging remark, lost his composure entirely. Once out in the street again, he was able to pull himself together and scolded himself roundly. But he could never summon up courage to present himself to the master again.

Beethoven, in any case, was fond of playing this work with his nephew Karl, and it may have been the only composition of Schubert that he knew until he made the discovery of Schubert's songs at the very end of his life.

The "French Air" of the variations is a square-cut tune of slightly antique cast which Schubert found in the library at Zselis. The time-signature of 4/4 is kept intact throughout the eight variations, although the tempo is slowed down in the seventh variation. The chief liberty is in the freedom of key, which although probably suggested by the example of Beethoven's Variations in F, opus 34, is not usual for the period. While the work is not especially venturesome for the most part, the finale has two unexpected and perfectly Schubertian modulations that deserve to be quoted:

Charming as these variations are, they cannot hold a candle to the next set in A flat, opus 35, which date from the second visit to Zselis. By that time Beethoven's tremendous "Diabelli Variations" had appeared, and there is evidence of Schubert's close study of them in the scherzo of his A minor piano sonata. Schubert had also taken Bach's "Well Tempered Clavier" to Szelis with him, and this work too may have played a part in the development of Schubert's variation style.

These A flat Variations were highly esteemed in Schubert's circle during his lifetime, and there are many references to them in letters and diaries of the period. In August of 1824 Schubert wrote from Szelis to the painter, Moritz von Schwind: "I have composed a grand sonata and a set of variations for four hands, the latter of which are having a particularly great success here; but as I do not wholly trust the Hungarians' taste, I leave it for you and the Viennese to decide." For his part, Schwind writes early the next year to a mutual friend: "These new variations for four hands are something quite extraordinary. In eight pages they are quite independently and vitally developed, and yet each again seems to reveal the theme."

With this judgment we can readily concur, and indeed, these variations are the finest independent set that Schubert ever wrote. The theme, with its two upbeats, suggests a slow-paced gavotte:

The eight variations alternate a lyrical and brilliant style, and the sixth, with its rushing sextuplets, attains a great momentum. The following variation, the slowest of the set, transforms the theme with exotic and slightly dissonant harmonies. Notice the intensely Schubertian modulations of the middle section:

(If you try this at the piano, be sure to observe the *pp* marking, and listen intently to the ensemble.) The finale is lighter in style, and although in 12/8 time has something of the easy-going and melodically inventive character of a Schubert waltz. The same modulation of the earlier set finds an echo in this finale, but with the minor second sustained this time:

Another set of variations that deserve mention here are those on a theme from Hérold's opera *Marie,* which date from the last year of Schubert's life. The opera had just been produced with great success in Vienna, and Schubert may have written these variations with an eye toward ready publication. The theme is charming, and its structure, with its clearly differentiated phrases, makes it ideally suited for variations. This work puts us in mind of some of Mozart's similar *pièces d'occasion;* although it is slight in intention, it is masterly in execution and delightful in effect.

That this work did not miss its mark with contemporary audiences may be attested to by the following review from the Leipzig *Allgemeine Musikalische Zeitung* for February 6th, 1828:

> . . . . we declare these variations to be the best of his that have so far come our way. The theme is at once captivatingly treated, and yet with the greatest simplicity. All the variations are mutually intertwined, diversified, and rich without affectation.

Of Schubert's other sets of variations, opus 82, number 2 is a set that first appeared in 1860, and whose authenticity has been questioned. The theme is obviously derived from the Russian tune that Beethoven used in one of his sets of variations, and it is possible that only Schubert would have been naive enough to copy his model so directly. Very likely it is an early work, quite agreeable in its florid pianism. This is Schubert testing his muscles, but not his wings.

The only remaining set of variations among Schubert's four-hand music is opus 82, number 1, which although published as a separate set was actually written as part of a three-movement suite, of which the Divertissement, opus 63, is the first movement, and the Rondeau Brilliant, opus 84, number 2, the finale. Future publishers of Schubert's four-hand music would do the work a great service by restoring it to its original form instead of keeping the present opus numbers, which were only the expedient of the publisher hoping for an easier sale by publishing it in separate sections.

Taken as a whole, this three-movement Divertissement richly deserved to be rescued from obscurity. The first movement begins as though it were going to be another of Schubert's marches, but this time Schubert feels impelled to develop it into a full-length movement in sonata form. Although it keeps a rather light march quality throughout, it is a most characteristically and unmistakably Schubertian piece, overflowing with brilliant and graceful passages for the two pianists.

The variations that make up the slow movement are the pearls of the work. There is something about the key of B minor that seems to have touched a special note in Schubert, as in the first movement of the *Unfinished Symphony* and such songs as "Die Liebe Farbe," "Zuleika's Song" and "Der Doppelgänger," and the same note is struck here too. The theme begins like another march, but this time as though from a distant dream world. The variations are very simple, but the magical, unearthly quality is never lost, and at the end, as the tempo becomes slower and the mode changes to major, it attains a visionary tranquillity.

The last movement brings us back to earth again. If it is a march, then it is the march of children on a holiday. As often in Schubert's finales, he likes to spread himself out on the largest possible scale, even though inspiration may not follow along all the way. Here the mood is carefree and the scenery picturesque. This three-movement divertissement built on march themes is a type unique in Schubert's output.

Schubert left one other divertissement for four hands, much the better known of the two, the "Divertissement à l'Hongroise," opus 50. We have the testimony of Schubert's friends that he was fascinated with the Hungarian music he heard while on the Esterhazy estate, and although the Hungarian influence became a lasting part of his style, this is apparently the only work in which he attempted to reproduce actual folk melodies. The first of the three movements opens with a little tune that Schubert is said to have heard whistled by a servant girl:

Later on there is an amusing suggestion of the tremolos and glissandos of the "zembalon," a zither-like folk instrument:

Liszt was particularly fond of this work, and arranged it for piano solo, and in the middle movement, for orchestra. Possibly it may have been the cue for Liszt's own "Hungarian Rhapsodies," and like them it makes the most of the contrasting styles of Hungarian folk music. However, it is in Schubert's lightest vein, and its relative popularity in the generation following Schubert's death, before his greater achievement was known, may conceivably have contributed to a slighting estimate of Schubert's importance during that time. But it is a charming work all the same, and the ending, which becomes softer and softer till it almost seems to disappear with a smile, is Schubert at his most winning.

# Schubert
## The Sonatas
## and Fantasies

ALONG with the two Divertissements, Schubert's most extended works for piano duet comprise two sonatas and the great Fantasy in F minor, opus 103.

The sonatas are both fascinating works, dating from the quite different periods in Schubert's creative activity of the two summers at Szeliz in 1818 and 1824. The first is a youthful work, which calls to mind such lovely early things as the little *Symphony No. 5* in B flat, while the second, known as the "Grand Duo," is one of the great works of his maturity, fully on a level with the last two symphonies, whose companion piece, some have maintained, it really is.

The first sonata in B flat, opus 30, while relatively little known, is a delightful piece that richly rewards a closer acquaintance. It is a most characteristic example of Schubert's early style, somewhat four-square in its phrasing, not yet free of reminiscences of Mozart and early Beethoven, but already filled with wonderful Schubertian melodies and modulations, and imprinted with what Tovey has called Schubert's "peculiar delicacy." After a brief pianistic flourish for the first player, the work opens with this theme:

With its little flurry of sixteenth notes, this tune somehow recalls the opening of Beethoven's Spring sonata for violin, opus 24. But if there is early Beethoven here, and a feeling of Mozart and Haydn, it could still be nothing but Schubert, and more specifically, Schubert of the early years. And what a wonderful feeling Schubert already has for the piano duet medium; there is not a note too much or too little. Although this excerpt could actually be played by a single pianist, it is quite clearly piano duet music and nothing else.

Could this movement perhaps have been in Schubert's mind when in the last year of his life he came to write his great B flat solo piano sonata, beginning with this melody?

Hardly has Schubert reached the orthodox key of F for his second theme than it dances away into D flat and other more distant keys before returning to F for a moment to finish the exposition. Soon we are traveling again through lovely Schubertian modulations in the development section, and before we know it, are back· to the recapitulation, which as so often in Schubert's early works, is quite regular and unvaried, and yet which seems not in the least perfunctory.

The slow movement is a pure gem, and in spite of the early date is great Schubert. In the affecting simplicity of the opening theme it is akin to Schubert's first great song cycle, "The Maid of the Mill," which was to follow not much later.

As so often in the songs, Schubert changes the mode of the theme when it returns later on, in this case from minor to major, and some-how it is even more poignant in its new form.

The finale is charming too, but as is so frequently the case with Schubert, he has exhausted his creative energies on the opening move-ments, and does not wish to wait, as Beethoven might have, for another day to renew his inspiration. The work must be finished at once, and so it is, but the finale is not quite on the same level as the rest of the work.

With the "Grand Duo" in C, opus 140, we find the mature Schubert at the height of his powers, and this work takes its place among the greatest of his compositions. There is a tradition that the "Grand Duo" is the piano reduction of a lost symphony, a tradition which originated with Schumann, who reviewed the work on its first publi-cation in 1838, ten years after Schubert's death.

> . . . The Duo, especially (which I regarded as a symphony arranged for the pianoforte until the original manuscript, which by his own hand is entitled "Sonata for four hands" taught me otherwise), still seems to me under Beethoven's influence. And in spite of Schubert's manuscript I still hold to my own opinions about the duo. One who writes as much as Schubert does not trouble too much about titles, and thus he probably hastily entitled his work "sonata" while "symphony" was what he had in mind. Then, to give a more everyday reason for my opinion, it is probable that when his name was only beginning to be known he was more likely to find publishers for a sonata than for a symphony. . . . We hear the string and wind instruments, *tuttis,* a few solos, the mutter of drums; and my view is also supported by the broad sym-phonic form, even by its reminiscences of Beethoven's sym-phonies, such as, in the second movement, that of the Andante of Beethoven's Second, and in the last, that of the finale of Beethoven's A major symphony. . . . With this conviction we should take up the duo. It is not necessary to seek for its beauties; they win us the oftener we hear them; one cannot help loving this loving poet.

The great violinist Joachim orchestrated this work with the advice and encouragement of his friend Brahms, and Tovey, in his essay on Joachim's version of the Grand Duo, strongly supports the thesis that this work is really a symphony. However, many Schubert scholars, such as Alfred Einstein and Maurice Brown question this assumption, and indeed, it is hard to believe that this work is anything but what it purports to be, a sonata for piano duet. Notice how casually it starts:

When Schubert is writing a symphony you can sense it immediately from the opening notes. But this theme has nothing symphonic about it—it *feels* like a piano piece. It is true that before long, in the transition section that leads to the second theme, there are intimations of an orchestral style:

And yet this is orchestral only in the sense that Schubert frequently approaches an orchestral quality within the framework of his chamber music or his piano style. The "Wanderer Fantasy" for piano, opus 15, for example, is full of just such orchestral sounding passages, and so is the great G major string quartet, opus 161.

The second theme of the "Grand Duo," having just arrived in the key of A flat, soon approaches its proper key of G by way of the delicate passage of pianistic filigree work that we quoted earlier in Chapter II. And note, by the way, the melting modulations in the passage following that leads to the end of the exposition.

The development section is not overly long in comparison to the exposition, but it is long by virtue of its richness of content and elevation of style. The recapitulation moves through some beautiful new modulations as the material is recast to return to the home key, and the movement ends with a powerful coda that rises for a moment to a quasi-orchestral climax before subsiding at last with an almost Brahmsian glow.

The slow movement begins with a theme of touching simplicity:

As it continues, we come upon those echoes of Beethoven that have struck Schumann and almost everyone else who has studied the work. And yet, somehow, the reminiscence of Beethoven in no way affects the Schubertian quality of the movement; it has in a way, something of the same function here that, for example, the quotation of "Frère Jacques" has in the slow movement of Mahler's *First Symphony*. After the first moment of surprise it seems inevitable, for it has taken on an entirely personal flavor in its new context. Indeed, if the first movement has a little of a Brahmsian cast, then this movement curiously enough seems almost to prefigure Mahler not only in the quality of its quotations, but in a feeling of unlimited spaciousness, and sometimes even in harmonic color. Witness this passage toward the end:

Or even more, this one:

The scherzo which follows has been very aptly called by Tovey one of Schubert's "grandest grotesques." Superficially this movement too seems orchestral in character, and it might well have been the ancestor of more than one of Bruckner's scherzos. And yet there is something in this particular type of "orchestral" sound that is purely pianistic. It is marked by a certain percussive dissonance that comes off magnificently on the piano. Take these splendid discords, for example, that appear just before the close of the scherzo:

The trio, based entirely on one unyielding rhythm, is mysterious, eerie, and cavernous in sound, truly a unique movement in Schubert.

The work ends with one of those rare finales in Schubert where there is, for once, no sense of falling off. The delightful opening theme seems to have a little trouble deciding if it is in A minor or C major:

In spite of the engaging quality of its themes, this movement is of serious intent, filled with a tremendous, driving, rhythmic vitality. There are orchestral moments in this finale too, as in the rest of the work, within the framework of a piano style. And here again are some of Schubert's magnificent percussive dissonances:

It is curious how in each of the movements of the "Grand Duo," Schubert seems to anticipate a later nineteenth-century composer—Brahms, Mahler, Bruckner—each of whom adored him. And in this finale too there are premonitions of another later nineteenth-century Schubert idolator, the Bohemian Dvorak. This phrase from the second theme could have come right out of one of the "Slavonic Dances":

Certainly the "Grand Duo" is known and appreciated by those who love Schubert, but it has by no means gained the general public acceptance that it deserves. It is a wonderful piece, altogeher worthy of those two other great C major works of Schubert's last years, the last symphony and the Quintet, opus 163. And like them it is absolutely *sui generis,* a work unique in Schubert's output.

With the beautiful Fantasy in F minor, opus 103, however, we are on familiar territory, for it is one of the best known and best loved of Schubert's works, and is probably the most often played of his four-hand compositions. Fortunately it is not too difficult technically for most amateurs to play, or at least to attempt, and it is overflowing with Schubert's loveliest and most beguiling melodies. If, as Schumann has suggested, the "Grand Duo" was written under the shadow of Beethoven, then this fantasy belongs under Mozart's star, for not only is its form derived, if somewhat distantly, from Mozart's great fantasies in F minor for organ and C minor for piano, but its very Schubertian opening theme is actually a harmonic variation of the opening theme of Mozart's G minor symphony: *

After a restatement of the theme in F major, the minor returns for a bold and powerful transition theme, which leads, however, only to a slightly varied restatement of the opening theme, this time in D flat minor. Another appearance of the transition theme, this time in A minor, leads to a final return of the opening theme in the tonic key of F minor. There is a serene and peaceful coda in the major which is based, surprisingly enough, on a transfigured version of the motive of the transition theme.

This movement, or perhaps we should say this section, for it is not quite long or varied enough to stand as an independent movement, leads directly into a new section in the unexpected key of F sharp minor, a Largo in a strong assertive style, based on a powerful dotted rhythm which calls to mind the "French overtures" of the baroque period, or perhaps even the opening section of Mozart's F minor fantasy. This passage breaks off for a moment into a lyrical interlude with this melody

which we would have been tempted to call redolent of the golden age of Italian opera, if Schubert could only have known it. Suddenly the

* If you are interested in tracing this kind of unconscious musical reminiscence, then transpose the Fantasy up to G minor or the Mozart symphony down to F minor, and make allowance for the notation in quicker bars in the Mozart and the absence of an introduction, and you will find that both works follow the identical harmonic pattern for the first sixteen bars of the Schubert, or the first twenty-four bars of the Mozart.

opening theme is back again, this time in a mysterious and unexpected *pianissimo,* before the section closes with a *fortissimo* extension of the powerful dotted rhythms of the opening.

Again without a break, this slow section leads directly into an *allegro vivace,* a brilliant and scintillating scherzo, with a trio marked by mysterious rushing passages and sudden accents. If you wish to make the most of the hushed excitement of the trio, remember the "vivace" of the tempo direction. The main body of the section sounds well enough at any tempo, but the trio can be a little tame if it is taken too slowly.

Although this is the only section of the work complete enough to stand as an independent movement, Schubert again leads without a break into the finale, which turns out to be a return to the lovely opening theme of the first section. This time, however, the bold transition theme turns into a fugue, which builds up into a surging coda, and the work closes with what seems almost a solemn, grief-stricken sigh.

It is curious that there was a time when Schubert used to be regarded as lacking in mastery of form. And yet in this wonderful fantasy, as well as in the two other great fantasies of his mature years, the "Wanderer Fantasy" for piano, and the fantasy in C for violin and piano, he has in effect created virtually a new musical form of his own. Although its origins are to be found in Mozart's fantasies, particularly the C minor fantasy for piano, Schubert's form has nothing of the sometimes sketchy and improvisatorial quality of Mozart's fantasies. This form, as Schubert used and developed it, marks one of the first important experiments in breaking away from the sonata form in a larger work, and it would be hard to overestimate the influence Schubert's fantasies have had on later attempts to develop new musical forms independent of the sonata form.

If we knew only these three great fantasies of Schubert's maturity, we might have been inclined to believe that the form came full blown to Schubert's mind. But actually, they were preceded by three early fantasies for piano duet dating from Schubert's thirteenth, fourteenth and sixteenth years. Although these early fantasies are not included in most standard editions of Schubert's four-hand music, they are found in the Henle edition as well as the complete Schubert edition published by Breitkopf and Härtel and reprinted by the Dover Press. These early compositions are not actually strong enough to stand in their own right as examples of Schubert's work, and are so loosely organized as to be hardly performable; indeed not one of them even ends in the key in which it started. But they are each of them absorbing works to study and play for those who love Schubert's music and are interested in the early stages of his development.

The first is inordinately long, filled with interminable changes of tempo, key and mood, in which the boy Schubert seems to be improvising as he goes. The contrast between the childhood works of Schubert and Mozart is remarkable—where Mozart is always the complete master by dint of limiting himself only to what he can handle, Schubert's childhood imagination seems to know no bounds. He achieves his mastery by jumping headlong into the ocean and learning to swim as he goes along. The second fantasy marks a remarkable advance between the ages of thirteen and fourteen; it is considerably shorter and shows a propensity for contrapuntal experiment. By the time of the sixteen year old fantasy, Schubert is only a year or two away from such masterworks as "Gretchen am Spinnrade" and "Der Erlkönig," and the piece is filled with many fine ideas and beautiful moments, particularly in the slow movement, which Schubert calls *andante amoroso*.

If the three fantasies of Schubert's boyhood are not performable in their own right, they still offer a fascinating glimpse into the process of Schubert's development into a great composer. And without them we should never have had the wonderful F minor Fantasy, for many of us the loveliest work in the entire piano duet repertory.

# VII ❧ Schubert
## The Smaller Pieces

A MUSICIAN who approaches Schubert's smaller piano
duet compositions for the first time is in somewhat the same position as
when he first becomes acquainted with Bach's cantatas. There are so
many of them, and they all seem so wonderful, that one is likely to
be overwhelmed by an embarrassment of riches. In the three volumes
devoted to Schubert's duets in the complete Breitkopf and Härtel
edition, an entire volume is given over to the marches alone, and then
there are innumerable polonaises, rondos, ländler, overtures and miscellaneous pieces. Unless one has the time to become a specialist, there
is a danger that one may acquire only a haphazard acquaintance with
these works and miss a great many beautiful things.

Let us see if we can put a little order into this profusion. Perhaps
it might be well to begin with the largest and most ambitious single
movement among Schubert's smaller pieces, the allegro in A minor,
opus 144, which was given the title of *Lebensstürme*, or "Life's Storms"
by its first publisher, Artaria, when he issued it posthumously in 1840.
This remarkable work dates from 1828, the last year of Schubert's life,
and is no doubt less known than it deserves to be because of its
incompleteness. In spite of its length, it is clearly only the torso of a
larger work, the first movement of what would have been, if Schubert
lived, a third sonata for piano duet continuing the series begun with
the sonata in B flat, opus 30 and the "Grand Duo."

The piece is a bold, impassioned sonata form written on Schubert's largest scale, and there are moments in it that seem to suggest new directions Schubert might have explored had he lived longer. Consider for example the extraordinary freedom in the treatment of the key of the second subject. The work opens with a powerful and vigorous theme in A minor, almost symphonic in style:

As is frequently Schubert's habit when he uses the sonata form on a large scale, the opening theme is continued at some length and includes some hints of a development and some variety of modulation before Schubert is ready to lead into his second theme. But notice how he goes about it. We have come to a pause on the chord of the dominant seventh, and the bass is left unaccompanied to sound a low E, the keynote of the chord in octaves in a syncopated rhythm. Slowly it moves down the notes of the chord, from E to D and to B, and at last in a whisper to the low G sharp, the third of the chord. Ever so softly above it (Schubert has marked it *ppp*) we hear the chord of G sharp major, and a new theme is softly and magically intoned in this unexpected key, which is actually the mediant of the dominant.

We have noticed how in the "Grand Duo" Schubert introduces his second theme for a moment in the foreign key of the lowered sixth (A flat as related to C) before leading into the normal key of the dominant for the statement of the second theme. Here the second theme is given out in its entirety in the even more strangely distant key of G sharp major, written enharmonically of course in A flat, before leading at last by means of the same solo bass line to the key of C, the normal key of the relative major, for a full restatement of the second theme. This time that theme is embellished with the exquisite filigree work of a variation in the uppermost part while the melody is given out in the left hand of the primo part.

The development section is vigorous and exciting, much more closely knit and carefully organized than is customarily the case in

Schubert at the Piano (detail of Leopold Kupelweiser's water-color).
*Editions du Seuil*

Schubert's earlier works. On the return, the first theme is subjected to new development as it leads to the second theme, now appearing in the key of F before returning in its delicate variation form to the home key of A major. A short but powerful coda brings this striking movement to a close. By the time we have reached the end of this piece it has generated enough energy and excitement to require a slow movement to follow it to release the tension. What he have heard is only the first act of a tragic drama, and the sense of incompleteness that it arouses is even sharper than in the case of the *Unfinished Symphony*.

Schubert has left another extended movement in the key of A, also dating from the last year of his life, the lovely rondo, opus 107, and the similarity of key has suggested to some commentators the possibility that it might have been intended to be part of a sonata of which the *Lebensstürme* would have been the first movement. But the rondo is so different in mood and style that one is inclined to doubt it, and in any case, Otto Deutsch tells us that this piece was specifically written at the request of the publisher, Artaria, who issued it in the same year, shortly after Schubert's death.

This rondo, in any case, is one of the most delightful and accessible of all Schubert's duet compositions, and is probably the best known among them after the fantasy in F minor. Its ingratiating opening theme gives us something of an idea of the beguiling nature of the piece:

It is pure gold throughout, and if there were only space we should be very much inclined to quote each theme as it occurs. But at least notice this subsidiary theme in F sharp minor, with its unusual disposition of keyboard sonority, as the tenor line takes the melody, sounding out above the repeated chords of the upper part, all on a level of *pianissimo* and softer:

This charming piece is not quite as easy as it appears on the first page, and it may require some practice on the part of both players in order to do it justice. But it is well worth the trouble, for it is among the loveliest of Schubert's smaller works.

Schubert has left one other rondo for piano duet, that in D major, opus 138, known to us by the title given it by its publisher, *Notre amitié est invariable*. In contrast to the rondo in A, this is an early work, actually one of the very earliest in the canon of Schubert's duets, for it was written even before the first trip to Szeliz, from which the flowering of Schubert's duet compositions first had its beginning. This rondo is hardly one of Schubert's more serious compositions, and its easy going *gemüthlichkeit* gives it something of the character of a salon piece. But slight as it is, it still possesses many of the salient features of Schubert's duet music, the exquisite delicacy of feeling for a chamber music style, the freshness of the modulations, and even in one extended passage toward the end, the crossing of hands between the partners.

Although it is not so indicated, the rhythm of this piece is that of a polonaise, a dance form that was particularly congenial to Schubert. As a matter of fact, Schubert with his ten polonaises, is, along with Chopin, one of the most prolific composers in this form. But since Schubert's polonaises are all for piano duet, they are practically unknown, although they contain some of his freshest and most delightful ideas.

We are likely to think of the polonaise as a specifically Polish dance, no doubt because of the peculiarly national stamp that Chopin has given it. But actually it is, along with the waltz and the minuet, one of the hardiest and most internationally practiced of all the dance forms. Bach and his contemporaries were fond of using it—the polonaise from Bach's B minor suite for flute and strings is a typical example of this period—and it flourished through the times of Mozart, Beethoven and Weber, all of whom left splendid "alla polacca" movements, until it reached its apotheosis in the hands of Chopin. But, throughout, it retains its essential character of a formal and ceremonious dance, almost as though it were a pompous march in three-quarter time, and always it maintains its characteristic cadence on the last two beats of the final bar of each phrase.

Schubert has a fine feeling for the character of the dance, and the polonaises are among the most charming of his smaller pieces. All ten date from the two visits to Szeliz, the first four of opus 75 from 1818, and the remaining six of opus 61 to the summer of 1824. (The reversal of the opus numbers is of course due to the fact that the second set was published first.)

The youthful Schumann was transported with enthusiasm when he first discovered these polonaises, and he describes them poetically in his diary as "downright thunderstorms, with romantic rainbows." They were the direct inspiration for one of the most striking of Schumann's earliest compositions, a similar set of eight polonaises for piano duet, written in 1828, which were to serve as a kind of source book for Schumann's first great masterpiece, the "Papillons," opus 2.

Knowing Schumann's fascination with these pieces, it is curious how almost Schumannesque certain passages of them seem to us now. Witness, for example, these measures from the polonaise in F, opus 61, number 2:

Or this touch of Schumann from the trio of the polonaise, opus 61, number 5:

In spite of the brilliance of these dances, they never for a moment exceed the limits of Schubert's most delicate chamber music style. The later set, opus 61, perhaps marks some advance in richness and maturity of style, but they are delightful, one and all.

If Schubert felt that the piano duet rather than the piano solo was the natural vehicle for these spirited dances, then evidently he must have had the same feeling about his marches, for they too appear only in his duet and not in his piano solo compositions. As with the polonaises, Schubert wrote a set of marches for each of the two summers he spent at Szeliz, but where the series stopped there for the polonaises, he continued to compose and publish marches for the rest of his short life. After the first two sets of marches, the "Trois Marches Heroiques," opus 27 dating from 1818 and the "Six Grandes Marches," opus 40 dating from 1824, the series continues with the gay and delightful "Marches Militaires," opus 51; and then with a group of two very large and almost orchestral marches written in 1825 to commemorate, of all things, the death of Alexander the First of Russia, and the accession of Nicholas the First. Finally, dating from 1826, are the two stirring "Marches Characteristiques," of opus 121, both in 6/8 time.

It is remarkable how within the framework of what might appear to be the rather limited form of the march, Schubert has been able to achieve an extraordinary variety, not only between the various sets, but in some cases, particularly in the six marches of opus 40, within the individual numbers of each set.

Of the three marches of the first set, opus 27, the first is the shortest and by far the most successful. The main section in B minor is in Schubert's most vigorous and spirited style, somewhat in the same vein as the splendid first *Rosamunde* entr'acte in the same key, and the trio in G is a fresh and naive melody that doesn't outstay its welcome. The other two marches of the set are considerably more diffuse, as in certain of Schubert's finales, where he seems to ramble on for ever and ever. The second march in C is particularly garrulous, and is marked by the unusual feature of a modulation to the subdominant rather than the dominant to end the first part, a rather doubtful experiment. But the entire piece modulates so freely that it becomes a little unorganized in regard to key. Perhaps if Schubert had been more self-critical, like Brahms, who destroyed more of his compositions than he kept, these pieces might not have been published. But then, on the other hand, if you are fond of Schubert, you may enjoy being acquainted with them.

The second set of marches, opus 40, marks a great advance over the first. Each of the six marches has a character of its own, and it is remarkable what variety Schubert has been able to achieve in style and mood between them. The first, in E flat, is a brilliant and effective *allegro maestoso,* a splendid opener for the set, with a trio of more lyrical and delicate character. Notice the charming ending of the first part of the trio, in which you can almost hear the *pizzicato* of the celli, and a delicate woodwind instrumentation in the upper part.

On the return of this passage at the end of the trio, the upper part is divided into alternating registers between the left and right hands.

The second march of the set begins with a jaunty, springing step in G minor, *forte* and *fortissimo,* but it turns out to be capable of moments of charming and unexpected chromaticism, *pianissimo,* such as the following:

The third march is in Schubert's most infectious Hungarian vein, and has a lovely, lilting trio in the major. The fourth, *allegro maestoso* like the first, suggests the brilliance of the full orchestra, and might well have been the ancestor of such progeny as Elgar's "Pomp and Circumstance" marches. The trio is a cheerful melody in G, with a delicate accompaniment in *pizzicato* style. The fifth, by way of contrast, is in a slow tempo, and has much of the character of a funeral march. Note the sombre, almost Brahmsian doublings, toward the end of the first section:

And by way of further contrast, the last march of the set is the gayest of all, a brilliant, spirited, irresistible tune in the bright key of E major.

Liszt was particularly fond of these marches, and made a number of arrangements of them for piano solo, very clever, but fiendishly difficult. Perhaps he may have been trying to do for the Schubert marches what he did for the waltzes in the "Soirées de Vienne," that is, choose a few to raise out of the anonymity of the collected edition, so as to make them more accessible to the general public. In the process of compressing four hands into two, and adding a number of original touches, Liszt has made them almost impossibly difficult. But if pianistic challenges intrigue you, they are well worth looking into.

The next of Schubert's marches has also been arranged, not by Liszt for piano solo, but by almost everyone else for almost every other possible combination, for it is that famous musical chestnut, the "Marche Militaire" number 1, in D. It is so familiar that it is hardly necessary to discuss it in detail, but the other two marches that complete the set of opus 54 are also worth knowing. The entire collection is in Schubert's lightest and most "popular" vein, and the second march has much of the charm of the first. As can be seen from this quotation, it recalls the overture to *Rosamunde*—and what could be more delightful?

The last march of the set is even more salon-like and more popular in style than the other two, and in fact, it approaches dangerously close to the trivial. The melody of the trio may well be the most frivolous tune that Schubert ever wrote; it could have appeared in any of a dozen light operas by any of a dozen other composers, or perhaps you may find in it a touch of Sousa or of Edwin Franko Goldman:

With the next two marches, opus 55 and 66 written for the funeral of Alexander the First of Russia, and for the coronation of his successor, Nicholas the First, we find Schubert in a very different mood. They are serious, ambitious, almost orchestral in manner, and rank with the finest of his four-hand compositions. None of Schubert's biographers seem to have any information as to what might have occasioned Schubert's commemoration of these historical events across the steppes of Russia, but Alfred Einstein suggests the possibility that Schubert might have been hoping for some token of Russian generosity. Although we do not know if this generosity ever materialized, we do know that instead of some trifling *pièce d'occasion* Schubert produced two splendid works in his best style.

The Funeral March, opus 55, is the shorter of the two pieces, quite straightforward in form, and simple and solemn as befits the occasion. But remember all the same, when you play it not to take it too slowly; there must be only two beats to the measure, not four. The trio demands much in endurance from the second player, for he is called upon to imitate paintistically the thunder of bass drum in his left hand and the roll of the snare drum in his right, with hardly any respite throughout. But in spite of the monotony of the lower part, there is not the least monotony in the effect of the piece as a whole, for it builds up gradually with a powerful and irresistible momentum. Notice this characteristic modulation at the end of the first part of the trio as Schubert moves from A flat major to B minor and back:

The more extended "Marche Heroique," opus 66, marked *maestoso*, is, as the title suggests and the occasion demands, splendidly heroic in style. The form of the piece is rather curious. After the jubilant opening pages there is a trio in a lighter, almost dance-like vein. But at its conclusion there is no indication of a *da capo*; instead Schubert goes directly into what appears to be an entirely new march, marked *allegro giusto*. This march has its own trio, followed by a return to the *allegro giusto* section, written out in full. Then comes a lengthy coda, in which as though to make up for the absence of a return to the first march, there are reminiscences of it combined with figures of its trio. Although this is the most extended of Schubert's marches, it is not a bar too long, for Schubert's inspiration never flags for a moment. An orchestral setting of this march by Rimsky-Korsakoff was first performed in Russia in 1868, and some enterprising musical scholar or editor might do us a good turn by resurrecting it. With Schubert's unfailing melodic inventiveness and Rimsky-Korsakoff's brilliant orchestral flair, it might well be worth hearing again.

With the last of the series of marches, the two "Marches Caractéristiques," opus 121, we again find Schubert at his best. Both these marches are in 6/8 time, which imparts to them a characteristically gay and joyous feeling. The first has a scherzo-like quality, and we can well imagine that it might have served as the scherzo to a symphony if Schubert had wished to orchestrate it, and its trio in A minor is one of

Schubert's most lilting melodies. The second of the two marches is in very much the same vein, as brilliant and joyous as the first. Both together make a happy and fitting finish to Schubert's splendid and unique series of marches.

Liszt was particularly fond of the first march of opus 121, and arranged it both for orchestra and piano solo. The piano version is a rather free affair, with the first part of the march brilliantly adapted for piano, as only Liszt could do, and very few but he could play. However, with the entrance of the trio section, Liszt suddenly decides to change the tempo to *andante siciliano,* and surprisingly enough, the melody is equally delightful in this guise, although its character is changed completely. Then Liszt breaks off suddenly and introduces the trio of the second march of opus 121, now *un poco pui mosso, quasi allegretto,* and before we are done, he has thrown in snatches of three different marches from opus 40 before rounding off the whole thing with a return to the opening, *vivacissimo* and *prestissimo, sempre con spirito.* If anyone could play this piece, it would be an absolute stunner with which to finish a piano program.

Schubert left one more march for piano duet, almost like a footnote to the series. In the summer of 1827, he and his friend Jenger spent a brief vacation in Graz, staying with their hospitable friends, the Pachler family. Before leaving, Schubert promised to write a four-hand march for the Pachler's eight-year-old son, Faust, to play at his father's nameday later that year. Schubert was a little slow in fulfilling his promise, but after a little prodding sent it along with a note of apology for little Faust: "I fear I shall not earn his applause, since I do not feel that I am exactly made for this type of composition." To tell the truth, this little march is not quite in Schubert's most inspired vein, but it is at any rate the easiest thing he ever wrote for piano duet, and as such has made its way into a number of anthologies.

If Schubert evidently felt that the piano duet was the natural medium for his marches and polonaises, then it is equally clear that he found the piano solo the most natural form for his numerous waltzes and ländler. He must have improvised an infinite number of them for the friendly social gatherings and dances at which he liked to play the piano, and his friends have told us that when he was particularly pleased with something he played he would repeat it over and over until he had fixed it in his memory. These delightful dances were among the most immediately popular of Schubert's compositions to his own contemporaries, and eight lengthy sets of them were published during his lifetime, not to speak of a number of other sets, all equally charming, that were salvaged after his death.

Schubert did occasionally work out these lovely dances for the piano duet, and the complete Breitkopf and Härtel edition includes a little set of four ländler for piano duet dated July 1824, that are as fresh and delightful as his solo dances. In addition, the manuscripts of two additional four-hand ländler in G and E, dating from the summer of 1818 were found by Brahms in the private collection of one of his friends in 1872, and were first printed in 1909. The firm of Schott has gathered together all these separate dances for piano duet, and published them in a little volume which is very well worth owning.

Also included in this collection are Schubert's own duet version of two of the waltzes from the well-known solo collection, opus 33. Actually this particular set of waltzes, one of the most deservedly popular in the entire waltz series, was originally issued in a piano duet version as well as in the familiar solo version which Diabelli first published in 1825, and this duet version can be found in an old Litolff album of Schubert's four-hand music, although it appears nowhere else. One is tempted to speculate on the possibility that Schubert might even have first conceived the whole set for piano duet, for the solo version contains passages of piano writing that are not quite as idiomatic as Schubert usually is. Consider this passage from the first waltz of the set, for example:

Those octaves in the left hand are a little awkward for the solo player, and it is hard to think of another place in Schubert's piano music where he indulges in this kind of octave writing in the bass, although it appears often enough in his four-hand music. In any case, whoever made the duet version, whether it was Schubert or someone else, did it with the utmost tact and delicacy, and the set of waltzes as a whole makes an excellent addition to the duet repertory.

Like Mozart, Schubert also wrote a fugue for piano duet, and like Mozart again, it qualifies as duet music only by courtesy, being conceived not in terms of two players, but rather as a convenient means of writing a fugue without having to limit it to what can be done by two hands and ten fingers. Schubert's fugue is even a transcription to begin with, for it was written originally as an organ piece in a friendly competition with a younger composer, Franz Lachner. Passing by an abbey on a walking tour, and stopping to try the organ, they set each other the task of writing a fugue for the occasion.

Although Schubert was keenly aware of his limitations as a contrapuntist, and was planning in the last year of his life to study with the renowned theoretician, Albrechtsberger, his natural mastery of contrapuntal skills was entirely adequate to his needs, as the fugues in his choral works amply testify. If not written "to the manner born" like Bach's, his fugues recall Mozart's in their slightly formalistic approach to the medium. This fugue in E minor, opus 152, begins conventionally enough, but before it is over has wandered into some very pretty chromatic bypaths. However, since it is actually a transcription of an organ work, you may prefer to learn it in that version if you wish to play it.

Among the other transcriptions that find a place in Schubert's duet catalogue is a little allegretto in C, which was written first as a choral setting of the Benedictus, and even has the Latin words written into the duet manuscript. This piece dates from Schubert's boyhood, and is pleasant enough in a rather Haydnesque fashion. Curiously enough, although it is one of the least distinguished of Schubert's duet pieces, it has found its way into a number of anthologies, no doubt because (like the little march written for Faust Pachler) it is not too demanding technically.

A very special category in Schubert's output are his overtures, of which he composed a number during a brief period in his earlier years, around and shortly after his twentieth birthday. Most of them are for orchestra, and of the four that we possess among Schubert's duets, two are Schubert's own transcriptions of orchestral works; another suggests that it also is, although we do not possess the orchestral version, and only one was specifically written for piano duet. Schubert seems to have found this form a congenial training ground for orchestral writing at a time when it would have been difficult for him to get a symphony performed. As Schubert uses the form, it even shows a slight approach to a symphonic variety, for all his overtures begin with a somewhat extended slow introduction before settling down to the allegro proper, and they almost all finish with an independent coda in quicker tempo.

The two overtures in the Italian style in C and D are both transcriptions of orchestral works; that in C is particularly interesting, in that Schubert used it as a kind of sketch for his familiar overture to *Rosamunde*. The theme of the introduction is repeated almost exactly in the later work, and there are other features of the allegro that find an echo in the later work. The overture in D is an attractive piece too, and it was with one of these two overtures that in March, 1818, Schubert made his first public appearance in one of his own compositions, not in the orchestral version, but in the piano duet setting, performed in this case with four players at two pianos, the two pianos duplicating each other. Schubert provided two of the eight hands on this occasion, along with his friend, Anselm Hüttenbrenner, the composer, and a duet team of two sisters, who appeared in other duets on the same program. We can imagine the brilliant effect this kind of performance must have produced, and the critical notice, as reprinted in Otto Deutsch's "Schubert Reader" was as friendly as possible.

The overture in F, opus 34, is the only one we know to have been composed for piano duet, and the only one that was published in Schubert's lifetime. Schubert noted on the manuscript that it was "written in three hours in Josef Hüttenbrenner's rooms in the Burgerspital, and dinner missed in consequence." Certainly it is hardly a serious work, and Schubert's commentators have been rather condescending about it. But it is a work of charm and good humor all the same, and is perfectly enjoyable if you take it in the right spirit.

Perhaps the most attractive of the four overtures for duet is that in G minor, which is found only in the supplementary volume to the Breitkopf and Härtel edition of the collected works. Although it is clearly symphonic in style, we do not possess an orchestral version, and so we can only guess whether it is an arrangement of a symphonic piece now lost, or only a sketch of a symphonic piece that Schubert never got around to writing. But in any event, it is a delightful piece, as fresh and captivating as anything of Schubert's early style of this period, rather more Haydnesque than Mozartean, yet all the same Schubertian too, as a glance at even such a brief excerpt as this will show:

If some clever arranger were to take the time and trouble to orchestrate this little piece in the manner of early Schubert, it would certainly deserve, and might even find a place in the orchestral repertoire.

In the final supplementary volume of the Breitkopf and Härtel collected edition to which this G minor overture of Schubert was relegated when it did not find a place in the main body of the work, there is one other major duet piece of Schubert that deserves notice, his own transcription for piano duet of the overture to his opera, *Fierrabras*. Curiously enough, another arrangement of the very same overture was made by Czerny for a series of popular overtures put out by the firm of Diabelli; and it is a most interesting exercise to compare the two arrangements, which were written quite independently. From the first note to the last they are as different in conception and execution as can be imagined. Czerny of course was at the disadvantage of being obliged to stick to the music at hand, while Schubert, as the composer, was in a position to allow himself a little more freedom. But the comparison between the two settings provides a perfect touchstone between a good workmanlike job, and a creative exercise of the imagination. Czerny's arrangement is filled with notes—he feels obliged to put everything in, while Schubert, on the other hand, leaves more breathing space. Czerny prefers to put the orchestral tremolos into sixteenth-note tremolos in the piano, whereas Schubert usually transforms them into eighth-note figures, which gives his version a lighter, more chamber music style. This brief excerpt from the last page of the score will provide an excellent comparison between the two versions:

Czerny

Schubert

Notice how Czerny eternally doubles the higher register of the upper part, while Schubert saves such doubling for an occasional highlight. Czerny doubles much more heavily in the bass too, not only here but throughout the work. And notice also the lightness that Schubert imparts to the arrangement by allowing the quarter-note breathing spaces in the left hand of the primo part in the last two measures of this excerpt. Schubert's setting is ever so much simpler, but compared to Czerny's routine version, it comes to life in an amazing way.

VIII    *Weber and Mendelssohn*

AₗₜₕₒᵤGH we are likely nowadays to think of Schubert as the first great Romantic composer, music lovers of Schubert's day and throughout the nineteenth century would have considered Weber, rather, as the first great musician to strike a truly romantic note in music with his opera, *Der Freischütz* of 1821. If in our century Weber's star has not exactly fallen below the horizon, its brightness has unfortunately been diminishing gradually. But it would be a pity if we were to lose sight of Weber, or neglect his striking and sympathetic musical personality.

Weber has maintained his hold in the repertory with the overtures to his operas, *Der Freischütz, Oberon* and *Euryanthe,* and with that brilliant and unconventional experiment in concerto form, the beautiful *Konzertstück* in F minor. But our parents and grandparents would have known him by a host of other things, not the least of them being his music for piano. Weber himself was an extraordinary pianist, and his four splendid sonatas strike a new note in piano music, not only in their romanticism, but in their brilliant and characteristic piano technique. They, as well as his other piano pieces, are still very capable of being revived, as Schnabel and others have shown, and the finale of his C major piano sonata, or the "Perpetual Motion," as it is better known, is still a dazzler.

Weber wrote three delightful sets of pieces for piano duet, his opus 3, 10 and 60, each one of them well worthy of study and performance.

Hindemith has based one of his most successful orchestral works, the "Metamorphosis on Themes of Weber" largely on excerpts from Weber's piano duets, and it is a fascinating study to compare the two compositions. Hindemith has remained faithful to the spirit, and, even to a considerable degree, the letter of Weber's music, and duettists who go to the trouble of looking up the originals will not be disappointed.

Like so many other great composers, Weber was a child prodigy of remarkable gifts, and his earliest duet pieces, opus 3, are an extraordinary production for a boy of fourteen that need no apology of any kind. Weber is among those composers whose personal accent, once you know his music, is unmistakable, and even in his earliest compositions we can catch his tone of voice.

The first piece of Weber's opus 3, which incidentally has found its way into a number of anthologies, is entitled "Sonatina," and begins as though it were going to be a full-fledged movement in sonata form. There is a cheerful and pleasantly flowing opening subject in C, then a transition passage which leads at measure 24 to a charming second subject in the dominant key, and then to a full close which ends the exposition at bar 35. However, there is no repeat of the exposition, and we soon realize that there is to be no development section, for the following eight bars are simply a brief transition leading to a return of the opening theme. And then we discover that there is not going to be a recapitulation either, for at bar 54 we jump right into a coda which brings the movement to an immediate and humorous close, and yet a perfectly satisfactory one.

As Weber continues the set, we get the impression that he wishes to give us all the movements of a sonata, even if on a miniature scale for we next have a little slow movement in F, followed by a brief menuetto in B flat (unexpectedly marked *presto*), and the last movement of the set is, appropriately enough, a rondo in the home key of C. In addition Weber has introduced a second slow movement, a short set of variations in G as the fourth movement, followed by a march as the fifth, a tiny thing, but witty and effective. Weber seems to be following the pattern of the six-movement serenade used so often by Mozart his lighter works, and by Beethoven in his Septet, where we have two slow movements (one of them likely to be a set of variations) and two lighter movements (most often a minuet and a scherzo). Weber has kept each of his movements here within the smallest possible confines, but the total effect is altogether complete and delightful.

Weber seems to have been so fond of this scheme that he used it again, almost identically, in his next set of duet pieces, opus 10, dating from his twenty-first year. These pieces are far more mature stylistically, and although still rather short, are developed at somewhat greater leisure. The first movement of the new set is again in sonata form, and if slightly abbreviated, is still complete enough to stand as a sonata movement. Again the last movement is a rondo in the same key, but considerably more extended than in the first set. And again we have a true adagio movement, which is the fifth piece in the set, as well as a set of variations which appears third. Instead of a minuet, Weber has given us a brisk mazurka for his fourth piece, and as a foil to it, a very charming movement in siciliano tempo which takes its place as the second movement. A quotation from this siciliano would be in order, as an example of the charm of Weber's style in his young manhood, and of his perfect feeling for the duet medium:

Hindemith has used this piece as the basis for the slow movement of his "Metamorphosis," and has provided some charming touches of orchestration in the slight variations he has made on the theme on its return. But there is a certain quality of sweetness and grace about this piece that exists only in the original.

With the last of Weber's three duet collections, opus 60, we find him at the height of his mastery, and the eight pieces that comprise the set are each of them a joy. As in the other two sets, there is a hint that here too Weber may have conceived this group of pieces as a kind of free suite in serenade form, but this time he has treated the idea with much greater freedom. The work ends with a charming and easy-going rondo, but the one piece in sonata form is now placed second instead of first, although it has a declarative and rather *galant* style that would have been entirely suitable as the opening of a large work. The third piece is a slow movement and the fifth a siciliano, one of Weber's most charming inspirations. A minuetto appears as the first piece in the collection, and deserves its place of honor, for it is a delightful and masterly piece in the purest chamber music style, a true conversation piece as all chamber music should be. Instead of a mazurka, Weber has given us this time a dashing number in Hungarian style as his fourth piece. (Hindemith, by the way, has used this as the opening movement of his "Metamorphosis.") Again there is a march, a powerful and stirring piece in G minor. (Hindemith has transposed this piece to B flat minor for the finale of the "Metamorphosis.") And finally there is another set of variations which appears as the sixth piece, a perfect gem, written on perhaps one of the shortest themes a master ever used for variations, a tiny fragment of a melody of eight bars. But with what charm and mastery Weber has handled it. You can gauge Weber's advance as a composer by comparing the variations in his three collections of duet pieces; this one is treated with incomparably greater variety and mastery than the others. Notice the beginning of the seventh variation in which the melody is given to the tenor voice in the second player's part, while above it the first player breathes the most delicate harmonies:

Schubert must have known this piece, to judge from his own use of this kind of duet color. And the graceful second variation must have given Mendelssohn the idea for the first variation of his own set, opus 83a.

No matter what the vagaries of fashion, it is impossible to imagine that Weber's music will ever die. But he lives not only in his own music, but to a much greater extent than we are likely to realize, in the music of the composers who came after him. Chopin's early rondos and sonata, opus 4, for example, show many touches of the influence of Weber, and Wagner's earliest style grows as directly out of Weber as Beethoven's out of Haydn and Mozart. And perhaps most of all, Mendelssohn's youthful compositions are permeated with Weber's influence, even where we least suspect it. That exquisite masterpiece of Mendelssohn's boyhood, the overture to the *Midsummer Night's Dream,* is certainly as unique and personal a thing as was ever written by a seventeen-year-old, and yet the closing theme of the coda, which seems to cast a benediction over the whole work, is an echo of a phrase from the Mermaid's air in *Oberon.*

Here is Mendelssohn's theme:

And here is Weber's:

Speaking of the overture to the *Midsummer Night's Dream,* it is interesting that Mendelssohn himself made a version of the work for piano duet which is among the earliest examples of a type of duet arrangement that was to become so immensely popular later on in the century. As with Schubert's duet version of the overture to *Fierrabras,* it provides a perfect touchstone for the difference between an arrangement as a creative work of genius and a routine, professional job.

Mendelssohn must have made the arrangement at about the same time as he composed the work itself, for his friend and teacher, Moscheles, tells of hearing the overture for the first time in a piano duet performance in November of 1826, while it was only in July of that year that Felix wrote to his sister Fanny: "I have grown accustomed to composing in our garden; today or tomorrow I am going to dream there a Midsummer Night's Dream."

Perhaps it might be interesting to note some examples of Mendelssohn's unerring tact in transforming the work from an orchestral to a piano piece. To begin with, the entire notation has been changed from eighth notes to sixteenth notes.

Orchestra:

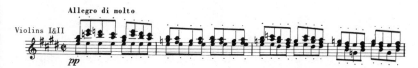

Piano:

It is curious how the sixteenth notes are exactly right for the piano, and yet would have been wrong for the orchestra. However Mendelssohn has kept the whole notes of the four opening chords intact—but of course they have fermatas in any case.

At the entrance of the second theme, notice how the repeated notes of the orchestral violas are transformed into an idiomatic piano style:

In this passage from the development section, notice the crossing of the hands in the primo part, which is the only possible way to achieve the lightness required for the two flutes of the orchestral version:

Mendelssohn, like Mozart, was fortunate in having an older sister who was a brilliant pianist and although Mendelssohn composed much less than Mozart for piano duet, the little he has left is filled with a love and understanding of the medium. There are only two works in the slim volume of Mendelssohn's duet music, neither of which he bothered to publish in his lifetime, yet both are precious additions to the four-hand literature.

The first is a set of variations, opus 83a, which was written together with the "Variations Sérieuses" for piano solo, and another less familiar set in E flat, opus 82, during a very brief period during the spring of 1841. Mendelssohn is among those composers of variations who prefer to start with a beautiful theme, rather than those like Beethoven or Brahms, who almost seem to make a point of choosing the most commonplace type of theme possible, as though to show what they can do with it. There is much to be said for the latter scheme in view of the possibilities it offers for growth and climax. But who can object when your theme is as lovely as this?

Tovey has remarked somewhere else of Mendelssohn that at times he can raise his most reckless prettiness to the height of great music, and he might perfectly well have been thinking of this theme. Each variation is a gem, written in the most natural and idiomatic duet style. In the seventh variation the melody floats above a gently moving accompaniment as sweetly and suavely as anything of Fauré:

The eighth variation ushers in a thunderstorm of mysterious rumblings and ghostly apparitions, leading to a last glimpse of the original theme. Then the storm dissolves into daylight, and the work ends on a lighter note with a sparkling finale. If you have the technique for it, this finale should be as light as air, and as quick as the wind.

This piece was published after Mendelssohn's death as opus 83a, while a version for solo piano appeared as opus 83. Most reference works list the solo version as the original form, and call the duet version an "arrangement," which just goes to show how easily an error gets picked up once it is allowed to pass. A comparison between the two versions indicates clearly that this work was conceived as a duet; the layout of the theme calls for two players, and Mendelssohn had to shorten it to adapt it for the piano alone. He made use of three variations that could be arranged for piano solo—although their order is no longer as effective as in the duet version—and has added two new ones to fill out the set. The duet version is finer in every respect, although the solo version is playable too, if you will only perform the new third variation with all the power at your command, and give your most poetic interpretation to the new fifth variation. Mendelssohn, like Mozart, has often been underrated as a composer because his music has been played badly; just as the "Dresden china" image of Mozart is obsolete, so too with Mendelssohn, you must not limit yourself to a nineteenth-century Biedermeyer approach. Play Mozart as though he were Beethoven, and Mendelssohn as though he were Brahms, if you want to do them justice.

Mendelssohn's other piece for piano duet, the "Allegro Brilliante," opus 92, is as different from the first as can be imagined. Where the variations are tender and intimate, the allegro is brilliant and virtuostic; not precisely theatrical, perhaps, but clearly intended · for the concert stage rather than the home. Mendelssohn dedicated this piece, like the fifth book of the "Songs Without Words," to Clara Schumann, and Grove tells us that he wrote it "expressly to play with his friend, Madame Schumann at her concert on March 31, 1841." What one would not give to have heard these two artists together! The Schumanns' youngest daughter, Eugenie, mentions in her reminiscences how her mother "aways spoke with the greatest delight of Mendelssohn; his legato, his playing altogether, she said, were perfect." Eugenie adds, "Felix Mendelssohn was the musician who appealed most to her as a human being, she had loved him truly; the remembrance of him could still bring a light into her eyes."

In the same key and time signature as the *Italian Symphony,* the "Allegro Brillante" recalls some of the verve and high spirits of that work, but in terms of a pianistic style that at moments almost seems to stretch the bounds of the duet style. Filled with rushing scales and flashing arpeggios, it is one of the most brilliant pieces in the repertory, and joins Mozart's sonata in C, K. 521 as one of those duet pieces that approach a two-piano style in their virtuosity. But in spite of appearances, it is not really quite as difficult as it seems; if your technique is reasonably sound, you should be able to master it with a little practice.

The second theme, which is given to each of the players individually at some length, is in Mendelssohn's most ingratiating mood:

The work begins like a sonata form on the broadest scale, but instead of a development, Mendelssohn returns at once to the first theme in a revised and shortened form, and the recapitulation then follows a normal course after the return of the second theme. Just before leading into the coda there is a humorous dialogue between the two players that is all but articulate:

and the piece winds up brilliantly with a short coda, *Presto!*

Mendelssohn left one other composition for piano duet, which is, however, virtually unknown, no doubt because it was written jointly with his friend Moscheles, and somehow joint musical collaborations never have been able to find their way into the repertory. It is a set of four variations on a theme of Weber, of which Mendelssohn and Moscheles each wrote two. However, since Mendelssohn also provided the introduction and almost all of the finale, the two lengthiest sections, his is certainly the lion's share of the work, although it must be said that Moscheles' contributions do him very great credit. The genesis of this composition is charmingly described in a book of reminiscences by Moscheles' son, Felix, a well-known painter of his day.

> . . . one evening they planned a piece for two performers to be played by them three days later at a concert my father had announced. The Gipsies' March from "Preziosa" being

chosen as a subject for variations, a general scheme was agreed upon and the parts distributed. "I will write a variation in the minor and growl in the bass," said Mendelssohn. "Will you do a brilliant one in the major and in the treble?" It was settled that the introduction and first and second variations should fall to Mendelssohn's lot the third and fourth to my father's. The finale they shared in, Mendelssohn starting with an allegro movement, and my father following with a "più lento." Two days later they had a hurried rehearsal, and on the following day they played the concertante variations, "composed expressly for this occasion" as the programme had it, "and performed on Erard's new patent-action grand piano forte".

Nobody noticed that the piece had only been sketched, and that each of the performers was allowed to improvise in his own solo, till at a certain passage agreed upon, both met again in due harmony. The *Morning Post* of the day tells us that "the subject was treated in the most profound and effective manner by each, and executed so brilliantly that the most rapturous plaudits were elicited from the delighted company.

After a brief, fanfare-like opening, Mendelssohn's introduction begins with this broad paced melody, accompanied in almost Chopinesque figuration:

Here is Mendelssohn growling in the bass:

And here is Moscheles' variation in the treble:

Even if Felix Moscheles hadn't told us, it would not have been too difficult to guess that the finale was Mendelssohn's, for it is in his most characteristic scherzando vein.

This work lay dormant for over a century, till just in the last few years it was revived by the American two piano team of Nelson and Neal, and shortly afterward repeated with great success by Frank Cooper and Raymond Lewenthal at the Butler College Festival of Romantic Music in Indianapolis. The work was originally issued for two pianos with optional orchestral accompaniment, and in a piano duet version, which is so completely recast as to make it virtually a piano duet composition. It is as though Mendelssohn and Moscheles were improvising the work anew as they wrote out the duet version (both of them were fantastic improvisers), and Mendelssohn has substituted an entirely new final page to finish off the coda in the duet version. Unfortunately both versions are out of print at present. Let us hope that some enterprising publisher will see fit to put them back in circulation soon. The duet version is at the Library of Congress, and they will send you a Xerox copy if you request it.

With this delightful set of variations, we might appropriately take a moment to glance at Mendelssohn's friend, Moscheles, who in his own day was almost equally celebrated. Moscheles was born early enough to have known Beethoven, who entrusted him as a young man with the piano reduction of his opera *Fidelio*. Moscheles was one of the most illustrious pianists of the day, and wrote copiously for the instrument, leaving almost as many works for piano duet as for piano solo. Among his duet compositions are two fine sonatas. opus 47 and opus 112, and a wealth of other things, all of them filled with charming and ingenious ideas. His opus 107, written for his young daughter, is a set of "Daily Studies" for piano duet, based on the scales in all the keys, in which one pianist (his daughter) plays the scales in various keys and tempos, while the other pianist (Moscheles) weaves around them all manner of fantastic things, including waltzes, mazurkas, tarantellas, barcarolles, and you name it—all turned out with the utmost taste and musicality. Moscheles' fame lasted well into the nineteenth century. As late as 1898, when Oskar Bie wrote his excellent study on the history of the piano and of piano music, he was able to give Moscheles more or less the same consideration as Mendelssohn. At that time, Mendelssohn's reputation was near its nadir, and one is inclined to suspect that Bie even has a slight preference for Moscheles, who gets two illustrations to Mendelssohn's one. But acute as Bie usually was, his judgment failed him for once at this point; certainly Moscheles was an admirable musician of genuine accomplishment, but the difference between him and Mendelssohn is the difference between talent and genius.

# IX ✣ *Schumann*

Hᴀɴs ɢᴀʟ, in a perceptive biography of Brahms, has divided his musical development into four periods corresponding to the seasons of the year. Perhaps it may be argued whether Brahms' music is best divided in this manner, since to many of us Brahms' last compositions have an autumnal rather than a wintry character. But if there is one composer whose music does correspond to the four seasons, then that composer is Schumann, for the last of his compositions just preceding his mental breakdown are shrouded in a wintry cloak of weakness and debility, while his earliest works are filled, as perhaps nothing else in music, with the freshness of earliest spring.

In Schumann's output for piano duet we can clearly recognize the four seasons of his style. Among the earliest of his compositions are a set of eight polonaises that antedate his opus one, in which he seems to be just discovering his gifts, while among the very last of his works are two sets of pieces for piano duet, opus 109 and 130, that bear witness to the tragic weakening of his powers in his last years. And between these extremes fall two other sets of duet pieces, the "Bilder aus Osten" opus 66, which show him in the full summer of his maturity, and an utterly delightful set of children's pieces, opus 85, written as a pendant to the immediately popular "Album for the Young," which represents, at its best, the rich autumnal quality of his later years.

Let us begin with a glance at his very first duet compositions, which belong to a series of youthful works that have been unearthed only in recent years, and have been given opus numbers in Roman numerals to distinguish them from the works with his own opus numbers. The eight polonaises, opus III were written in 1828, only a year or two before the composition of this first great masterpiece for the piano, the "Papillons," opus 2.

Along with the signs of musical immaturity that are evident in these early polonaises, there are also signs of a bold and imaginative talent, combined with a penchant for every kind of musical experimentation. Sometimes Schumann's harmonic experiments work brilliantly, while elsewhere they occasionally fall flat. But his extraordinary gifts are apparent on every page—you can almost feel the sparks of talent flying out in all directions.

It requires only the merest glance at these polonaises to see how directly they derive their inspiration from the example of Schubert's polonaises for piano duet, which Schumann adored. His friend of that period, Emil Fleissig, writes: "For Schubert—then in 1828 first becoming known—he developed a raving passion, and got hold of everything of his that was to be had. In the polonaises I had to accompany the bass." We have noticed in our discussion of Schubert's polonaises how some passages sound veritably Schumannesque; there are also passages of Schubert's characteristic harmonic liberty that may have provided the cue for some of Schumann's more doubtful experiments. Witness this passage from the trio of Schubert's polonaise, opus 75, number 2:

which must have tempted Schumann into progressions such as the following, where he seems to have overreached himself a little:

Following Schubert's example, where the polonaises are relatively brilliant and the trios quieter and more lyrical we find almost always that Schumann has reserved his more intimate thoughts for the trios of his polonaises. Each of the trios is given a title in French, suggesting a general mood or style, such as "La douleur," "La paix," and so forth. Here for example is the beginning of the trio of the sixth polonaise, "L'aimable," in which for the first time we can recognize Eusebius' shy and gentle smile:

Here is a typical example of Schumann's more brilliant style taken from the main section of the fourth polonaise:

In case this passage sounds familiar, the explanation will be apparent on comparing it with the following passage from the corresponding place in the eleventh of Schumann's "Papillons," opus 2.

Actually, Schumann has used these polonaises as a kind of musical sketchbook for his first great masterpiece, and if you want to measure the advance from the musical adolescent of 1828 to the master of 1829, then these two excerpts may prove illuminating. The first is from the trio of the seventh polonaise, which Schumann has entitled "La fantasie:"

And here is its transformation into one of the loveliest of the "Papillons":

After Schumann's death, Clara Schumann gave the manuscripts of his unpublished compositions to Brahms and Joachim for their advice as to what to offer to the public. Naturally enough, they felt at the time that these polonaises were too immature to enhance Schumann's reputation, and they wrote on the manuscript, "not for publication."

It was only in 1933 that Karl Geiringer, the custodian of the collection of the *Gesellschaft der Musikfreunde* in Vienna where the manuscript was kept, edited them and gave them to the firm of Universal in Vienna for publication.* Unfortunately this work has gone out of print, although you may perhaps be lucky enough to find a copy occasionally in a second-hand music shop. But these pieces form a fascinating collection, not only for themselves, but for what they portend, and certainly it must only be a matter of time before they are available again.

Schumann turned with such absorption to the solo piano in the next decade, and to other mediums in the decade following, that we do not find him returning to the piano duet until 1848, with the publication of the "Bilder aus Osten," opus 66. In the preface to these pieces Schumann writes that they were inspired by a reading of a series of free translations from the Arabic by the German poet, Friedrich Ruckert, in his *Die Verwandlung des Abu Seid von Zerug, oder die Makamen des Hariri.* But if Schumann hadn't told us, it would never have entered our minds to think of an Oriental connotation for these pieces. They are filled with the spirit of Schumann's most intimate German romanticism, and the organ-like opening of the last piece might almost have come out of the *Rhenish Symphony.* It is necessary to search very closely indeed to find the least trace of anything Oriental in this music. Could the gently swaying opening of the fourth piece perhaps be Schumann's Germanic conception of an Oriental maiden's sinuous dance?

Or could these unexpected progressions from the third piece possibly be Schumann's idea of Oriental harmony?

* Geiringer has undertaken to correct a number of Schumann's "mistakes," such as parellel fifths, etc., but has given us the original version in footnotes. In our musical illustration, we have restored the original readings in every case.

But Oriental or not, these pieces represent Schumann in the best vein of his later middle period. Perhaps the most remarkable thing about them is the rather full and heavy writing for the piano; one is tempted to imagine that Schumann may have originally conceived them as an orchestral suite, and feeling that a set of character pieces of this type was too light for symphonic treatment, decided instead to give them to us in this four-hand version. Nowhere else in Schumann's duet writing does he approach this frequently heavy-handed and almost turgid pianistic style, for which however, we can most willingly forgive him because of the great charm of the music itself.

Schumann's next duet collection, the "Twelve Four-Handed Pieces for Big and Little Children," opus 85, dating from the following year, is much more idiomatic pianistically. For the most part scored rather lightly, it is as fresh and charming as anything Schumann ever wrote in his life. Its existence was due to the immediate popularity and success of the "Album for the Young" for piano solo; the publisher felt that a similar work for piano duet would be welcomed and Schumann obliged with this little set of pieces. Like the original "Album for the Young," these pieces recall the verve and élan of Schumann's earliest work, but are written with Schumann's maturest musical mastery, and on a pianistic level that Schumann endeavored to keep as simple as possible. And like the "Album for the Young," again, this set opens a little slowly, as though Schumann were overly fearful of taxing his beginning pianists with anything too difficult. The first piece is a rather routine march, with very little sign of Schumann's genius, and the second piece, entitled "Bear Dance" is a whimsical idea, in which the second player has hardly more than a series of pedal point chords to reiterate.

But with the third number, the lovely "Garden Melody," Schumann stands before us to the life, and from there on the inspiration never falters. Notice how few notes Schumann needs in this piece to convey

Robert and Clara Schumann (lithograph by Hofelich). *The Bettmann Archive*

his warmest and tenderest romantic feeling:

It must be admitted that Schumann occasionally forgets himself in regard to difficulty, for some of this music is really not at all easy. The ninth piece, for example, "Am Springbrunnen," requires the utmost lightness of wrist and touch to do it justice, and the following piece, "Verstuckens," is not far behind in difficulty. But the last number of the set, the lovely "Abendlied" could be played by a child, or shall we say, two children, if there were only two children gifted with the musicality and the depth of feeling that this music deserves. This beautiful piece has made its appearance in a number of other guises; organists may recognize it from its inclusion in a number of organ anthologies, and in fact it does suit the organ beautifully and might very well be played in church. Joachim once used it as an intermezzo at an orchestra performance of Brahms' *Requiem,* and its beauty and inwardness of feeling must have made it entirely appropriate at this occasion.

With this entrancing set of pieces, certainly one of the most delightful things in the entire duet repertory, Schumann reaches the high point of his four-hand writing. This work was composed in 1849, and he was not to have too many good years left. The Third or *Rhenish Symphony,* which dates from the following year is the last major work in which we still see him at the height of his powers.* After 1850 there is a slow but steady decline until 1854, the year of his attempted suicide and his incarceration at the asylum in Endenich.

But it is remarkable that the last works show no decline in the beauty of his ideas, or even in their character; his growing weakness manifests itself chiefly in a lessening of the sustained power of concentration. Even his last major work, the violin concerto of the end

* The *Third Symphony* is actually the last of Schumann's four symphonies, for the so-called fourth is only a revised version of the Second Symphony of 1841.

of 1853 is filled with wonderful ideas. The strength and nobility of the opening theme suggest that it might well have matched the splendid piano concerto as one of the great works in the repertory. But Schumann can hardly sustain its power for more than a few lines. Where once there was certainty and strength, there is now doubt and hesitation. The slow movement too is filled with beautiful themes, but the finale, after a brave attempt at a gallant polonaise rhythm, falters tragically after a few moments.

The two sets of piano duet pieces that date from Schumann's last years, the "Ballscenen," opus 109 of 1851 and the "Kinderball," opus 130, of 1853, show these same characteristics of mingled beauty and weakness. Both sets are similar in conception and mood, being collections of characteristic pieces in various dance forms. Each set contains a polonaise, a waltz, an écossaise, and what Schumann calls a "Française," that is, a brisk, gigue-like dance in 6/8 time. In addition the later set includes a minuet and a round-dance, while the earlier set also contains a mazurka, a Hungarian dance and a second waltz, as well as a ceremonial "Préambule" by way of introduction, and a festive "Promenade" to conclude the set.

As we might expect, the earlier of the two sets shows greater spirit and energy. In 1851 Schumann was still capable of fine things, and from this year date the two violin sonatas and the third trio in G minor, all of them works of great beauty, although they fall short in strength and impact as compared to the masterpieces of the earlier days. The "Ballscenen" of 1851 is still a viable work, filled with excellent ideas, and given a thoughtful and careful interpretation is well worth playing.

By the time of the "Kinderball" of 1853 the weaknesses are much more evident—the unnecessary repetitions within a phrase, the lack of momentum, the inability to sustain an idea. The best piece of the set is a little waltz, in which we can still catch a glimpse of the old Schumann:

But in spite of their weakness, these last two duet collections, like the violin concerto, are precious to those who love Schumann. In the beauty and intensity of his work as a whole, in its immediacy of personal feeling, he struck a note entirely his own. How much poorer and emptier the world would have been if he had never lived!

# X ❦ *Brahms*

By the time Brahms was growing up musically, the piano duet was in the full tide of its popularity, and among Brahms and his circle there are innumerable references to duets and duet playing. Thus Eugenie Schumann, the youngest daughter of Robert and Clara, writes in her old age of the days of her girlhood: "We children all liked Brahms; we were in raptures about his serenades and sextets and never tired of playing them as duets." Or Brahms' friend, Ignaz Brüll, urges him to spend the summer at Ischl: "I have been looking forward to our walks, our pleasant coffee parties and much besides—and most of all to the playing of new duets." Or here is Brahms, in the spring of 1860, writing to Joachim: "These past days I have been setting my second serenade for four hands. Don't laugh! I was in a perfectly delightful mood; seldom have I written music with such pleasure."

To Brahms it was a perfectly natural thing to arrange his music for piano duet, and often his symphonies and other larger works were first heard in duet form before a group of friends or colleagues, occasions which might provide the opportunity for sympathetic criticism before they were given to the world. And it was for the medium of the piano duet that Brahms reserved some of the loveliest and most intimate of his works. The waltzes, for example, all took shape in his mind as duets. Both the first set of waltzes, opus 39, and the later "Liebeslieder," opus 52 and 65, were written as duets, although the latter sets used the duet as an accompaniment for a group of vocal soloists and were only later published for duet alone. The "Hungarian Dances" too, those delightful settings of the gypsy tunes that Brahms picked up on his tours with Remenyi and which first spread his fame around the world, were written as duets before being arranged for almost every other conceivable combination. And perhaps finest of all, the wonderful variations on a theme of Schumann, opus 23, were written as a piano duet and never appeared in any other form at all.

First in point of time are the variations, which date from 1861. Unlike the variations for piano solo on a theme of Schumann, opus 9, which were written during Schumann's lifetime and which gave Schumann much pleasure, even though he did not see them until after he was hospitalized, these variations for piano duet were written after Schumann's death, and have the character of a eulogy to Schumann's memory. The theme is Schumann's very last musical composition, which shortly before his mental breakdown he imagined was dictated to him by the spirits of his beloved Schubert and Mendelssohn—although as Geiringer has pointed out, it is actually an echo of the slow movement of his violin concerto.

The only possible sign of weakness in this theme is that it is a little short breathed; the cadence at the end comes a little sooner than we might have expected, as though Schumann lacked the strength to carry his musical idea to full completion. But it is a lovely thing all the same, imbued with Schumann's tenderest *innigkeit,* and this haunting melody inspired Brahms to one of the finest of his sets of variations.

The first variation delicately ornaments the theme without obscuring its outline, while the second is richer and freer, with a somewhat stronger rhythmic feeling which may be accented ever so slightly. Notice the powerful reserve of strength that Brahms keeps for the second half of this variation; it is marked *forte, più forte* and *fortissimo,* directions that must be faithfully observed. The third variation moves along faster in sixteenth-note triplets, but here the markings are *dolce* and *espressivo.* As a matter of fact, Brahms repeats these words a number of times throughout the variation, and for someone as careful of notation markings as Brahms, these indications are significant. This variation is in Brahms' loveliest vein, and these measures at the beginning of the second half will suggest something of its tenderness and warmth:

A note of foreboding appears in the fourth variation. It is in the minor for the first time in the set, and suggests the somber woodwind coloring of Brahms' orchestral writing, with a hint later on of an ominous muffled kettledrum, first in slow sixteenth notes, and then as a soft roll. The fifth variation in 9/8 time, *poco più animato,* moves to the brighter key of B major; it is as though a ray of subdued sunlight drifted through the clouds. The lower player states the melody first, as though in Brahmsian horns or cellos, while a triplet figure is exchanged between the lowest and highest registers. The sixth variation, *allegro non troppo,* introduces a note of strength and power—not the strength of the trumpets, but rather of the massed strings, leading in the seventh variation to this lovely interlude of gently shifting harmonies:

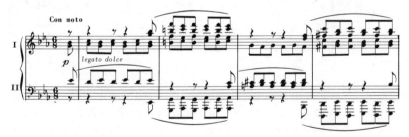

More passionate is the eighth variation, a momentary echo of a lilting Hungarian Dance. But the mood of the work is tragic, and the next variation, with its rushing scales and powerful dotted rhythm seems almost like a desperate battle against fate, as it closes into the final variation of a grave and measured march tempo. Above the somber rhythm of this funeral march, the original theme appears like a wraith, a last remembrance of Schumann, as the work sinks to a quiet and elegiac close.

Tovey has rightly called this composition one of Brahms' greatest and most poetic sets of variations, and it would be hard to account for its almost complete neglect, unless the reason is that it is written for piano duet and exists in no other version. But it would be impossible to arrange this work for any other medium without losing its intimate character. It must be played and known in its original duet form, but it is a treasure that will richly reward those who seek it out.

Brahms' next duet composition, the set of waltzes, opus 39, has given pleasure to innumerable music lovers as a piano solo, but the solo version really does not do it justice, as even a superficial comparison of the two versions will show. Here for example is the opening of the fifth waltz in both forms:

How much is lost in the solo version. And even where a single pianist can play all the notes, or most of them, as in the brilliant opening waltz, or the more reflective second waltz, it is still not quite the same thing. Inevitably there is a certain sense of effort, if not of strain, and there is a slight loss of spontaneity and ease in the first waltz, or, in the second, of graciousness and intimacy. But all the same, this is such a friendly and delightful work that we must be grateful to Brahms for making it at least accessible to solo pianists.

There is a considerable variety in the sixteen waltzes that make up the set; many are gentle and tender, and Brahms' favorite markings of *dolce* and *espressivo* appear frequently throughout. But some waltzes are more powerful, and in the fourth marked *appassionato,* with its suggestion of the violin's double-stopping, or in the first cadence of the eleventh, you can almost hear echoes of the "Hungarian Dances."

It is interesting that Brahms has transposed the last four waltzes of the set down a semitone in the piano solo version, no doubt because they lie more easily under the fingers of a single pianist with the additional black notes of the new keys. Thus the best known of the set, the charming folk-like fifteenth waltz, is familiar to solo pianists in A flat—always a congenial key for pianists, as Schubert knew very well. But once you have played it as it was first written in the key of A with its modulation to C sharp minor then the brighter key seems somehow the only right one for the piece. The last waltz is a little gem too; instead of ending with one of his brilliant waltzes Brahms has chosen instead to end on a quiet note, and this lovely little waltz seems almost to be saying farewell.

The two sets of "Liebeslieder" waltzes with vocal quartet, opus 52 and 65, or 52a and 65a in the version for duet alone, are quite different in style, and to those who knew them they are invariably special favorites among Brahms' compositions, as indeed they were to Brahms himself. It would be impossible to say that they are better than the waltzes, opus 39, but they are more expansive in mood and warmer in sentiment. No doubt much of their character is due to the fact that they are set to touchingly sentimental love poems of the poet Daumer, and indeed, they lose much apart from their texts, which in every case gives the clue to the understanding of the work. Although the piano duet accompaniments are virtually complete in themselves without the singers, they really lose too much without the voice parts to be entirely satisfactory purely as duets. Even though Brahms himself made the duet versions, they are in a sense only duet pieces by courtesy. But they are among the loveliest and most beguiling of all Brahms' compositions, and duettists should take the opportunity to become familiar with them, either with or without the voice parts.

As a pendant to Brahms waltz duets, perhaps we might say a word about the four-hand transcription that Brahms made of a set of Schubert waltzes that he found at the home of his friend Julius Stockhausen.

Manuscript of Brahms' *Variations on a Theme by Haydn, left hand page.*
*Collection of the Library of Congress*

The original version for piano solo had not been published when Brahms first saw it, but it is a charming thing in Schubert's best vein, filled with his characteristic and individual harmonic touches and modulations, and it so captivated Brahms that he made his own four-hand arrangement of it to give to Elise Schumann along with his own four-hand waltzes, opus 39. Brahms has handled the original with the greatest restraint, merely dividing Schubert's solo waltzes between the two players. Yet curiously enough, Brahms' arrangement seems to add something to it, and certainly we can take pleasure playing it in four hands as Brahms did. You can find it along with Schubert's own small portfolio of four-hand waltzes in a Schott album, and it is well worth knowing.

Although Brahms' "Hungarian Dances," published in two separate collections in 1869 and 1880, were the first compositions to bring him world-wide fame, they are sadly neglected today, and perhaps it is not surprising considering how hard it is to escape the association of those

Manuscript of Brahms' *Variations on a Theme by Schumann,* right hand page.
Collection of the Library of Congress

syrupy violins of salon orchestras that usually play these dances. Indeed, these gypsy dances, even in Brahms' own duet settings, sometimes almost seem to call for this kind of treatment, as at the beginning of the fourth dance of the first set, for example:

This approaches perilously near to "camp," and the first book generally, with its routine gypsy turns and cadences and its frequent tremolos, is a little hard to play nowadays except with tongue in cheek.

But the second book, published considerably later, is finer in every way. Even where Brahms is enmeshed in the gypsy style and permits himself a few tremolos, they are worked out with a more individual flavor and somehow sound more Brahmsian. Here for example is the beginning of the fourteenth dance, the fourth of the second book; close as it is in its Hungarian feeling to the dance quoted above, yet it is worlds away from it:

The second volume of the Hungarian dances stands somewhat in relation to the first volume as the second volume of the Paganini variations to the first; it is subtler, more mature, more delicately written in terms of piano style, and more Brahmsian altogether. Note the chamber music quality of the ending of the thirteenth dance, for example, and how charmingly Brahms has extended the last three-bar phrase to four:

Three of the eleven dances of the second collection are entirely Brahms' own, the eleventh, the fifteenth, and the seventeenth, and there is much in this second volume that deserves to be salvaged. But it was the first volume that proved to be so immensely popular in Brahms' day, and that led directly to the creation of a whole series of national dances. Dvorak's "Slavonic Dances" and Grieg's "Norwegian Dances" are the finest of these, as well as the best known, but among the many national dances that owed their existence to the success of Brahms' first volume are a series of Lithuanian dances by his friend, Herzogenburg, a set of Swedish dances by Max Bruch, and later on, two fine Finnish dances by Busoni, Scottish dances by Malcolm Arnold, and a charming set of three English dances by the song writer Roger Quilter.

Among Brahms' contemporaries, a word should be said for the gifted Hermann Goetz, whose unusual promise was cut short by an early death. Goetz left an opera based on Shakespeare's *Taming of the Shrew* that was a favorite of Mahler, a symphony that Shaw preferred to Brahms', as well as a series of chamber music works that include a very interesting sonata for piano duet which is at the New York Music Library. It is a work of great charm and refinement, influenced by Mendelssohn rather than Schumann, but with a very sweet and sympathetic note of its own, which you can recognize in this excerpt from the slow movement.

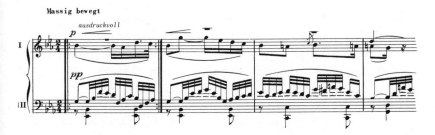

Among other contemporaries of Brahms who left sonatas for piano duet are his friend, Albert Dietrich, and the famous organ composer, Rheinberger. Less known than it should be, but filled with its author's genial personality is a sonata for piano duet by Anton Rubinstein, which like the two others, can be found at the Library of Congress.

Rubinstein adds his own brand of virtuosity to the piano duet medium as this excerpt from the scherzo will show:

For a long time Rubinstein's "Bal Costumé"—a delightful set of pieces suggested by the various characters of a masked ball—was extremely popular, and if you are lucky enough to come across a copy at a second-hand store, you will find it well worth having. Rubinstein is actually a better composer than he is given credit for nowadays, and you can find in his music the first stirrings of a characteristically Russian note of sadness and nostalgia that Tschaikowsky and Rachmaninoff were later to express with much greater intensity. The three concluding general dances of the "Bal Costumé" show Rubinstein at his best, and if you play over the waltz you will see where Tschaikowsky found the model for some of his most characteristic ballet waltzes. And the galop has such an irresistible sweep and vigor that it is easy to see how its composer carried everything before him as a pianist.

It would not be fair to omit mention of another duet composer, whose music like Rubinstein's was immensely popular in the last century, Moritz Moszkowski. A good deal of Moszkowski's duet music is still in print, particularly the Spanish Dances, and a charming set called "From Foreign Lands." Lightweight as it is, Moszkowski's music still has a winning appeal, is beautifully written for the piano, and has the merit for pupils of sounding more difficult than it is. In the catalogue of Stephen Heller are a set of waltzes, his only original composition for piano duet, and the talented and genial Karl Goldmark also has a set of lilting waltzes that can be found at the Library of Congress.

But the list of duet composers of the latter part of the nineteenth century would be far too long to even attempt to enumerate here, and most of them are not as fortunate as Moszkowski in still being in print. Adolf Jensen, for example, so highly spoken of by Oskar Bie, by Rowley, and by so many others—it will only be a matter of luck if you can still find his compositions in a second hand shop to judge for yourself. Or Joachim Raff—regarded as a master in his day—as indeed he was! Or the brilliant Scharwenka. Or so many more, whose music must await a Romantic revival comparable in scope to the Baroque revival of recent years, which has rescued so many minor but gifted eighteenth-century composers from anonymity.

# XI   *A Miscellany*
## Chopin, Liszt and a Few Others

I*T* MIGHT be a little paradoxical to speak of Chopin and Liszt as duet composers, for both were such consummate masters of the piano in their solo works that they had very little need or incentive to experiment with other pianistic mediums; and indeed their contribution to the piano duet is quite minimal. But even the little they did leave is of particular interest, and once we look into it we shall find, certainly in the case of Liszt, that there is somewhat more than we expected.

In his book-length catalogue of the complete Chopin *œuvre,* Maurice Brown lists only two early compositions for piano duet, both of them lost; a set of variations in F on an original theme, and a set of variations on an Irish national air of Moore in D. But since this work was published in 1960, the latter composition has been exhumed and published in Poland, and reprinted in the United States by the firm of Edward B. Marks. This set of variations is based on the following Neapolitan melody, which incidentally has also been used by Paganini in his "Carneval de Venise":

Chopin's sister, who after his death made a list of his unpublished compositions, referred to it as a set of variations on a national air of Moore, and we may infer that the youthful Chopin found it in a then well-known collection published by the Irish poet, where it appears set to a text beginning, "Oh come to me when daylight sets." The manuscript of this composition has come down to us in a sadly tattered condition with the first and last page missing, but the lost pages, which comprise the secondo part of the introduction and theme, and the primo part of the last variation, have been reconstructed with exemplary skill and tact by Jan Ekier for the printed edition.

According to Chopin's sister, the work dates from 1826 when Chopin would have been in his sixteenth or seventeenth year, and it is frankly a juvenile work of historical rather than musical interest. But if Chopin had not yet attained the personal idiom that he was to acquire in only a few years with the two piano concertos and the first of the études and nocturnes, it is remarkable in showing Chopin's precocity in handling the piano. In terms of piano style, there are touches that suggest the mature Chopin, as for example this charming filigree work in the primo part of the introduction:

Or again, this brilliant and individual passage work from the first variation:

The first slow variation in the minor, while not musically distinguished, already shows something of Chopin's delicate feeling for arpeggio figuration:

For anyone who loves Chopin this work has a special interest, not only as Chopin's only extant duet composition, but as a remarkable illustration of Chopin's early feeling for piano style.

The case of Liszt is somewhat more complicated, for although he left very little originally for piano duet, he did leave duet versions of some of his solo compositions which in a few cases deserve to be considered on equal terms with the solo versions; and he also made piano duet arrangements of many of his orchestral compositions, as well as of various works by other composers. Add to this Liszt's penchant for rewriting his compositions in various forms and mediums, often many years apart, and it can be seen that the problem of sorting out the Liszt catalogue is among the more difficult of musical tasks. We owe much in this field to the Herculean labors of Humphrey Searle, who has devoted a book to the subject, and to Felix Raabe before him, the author of the first comprehensive Liszt biography—but even they have not been able to prevent occasional errors from creeping in, and their catalogue of Liszt's duet music is not quite free of them. Raabe has an exhaustive six-page listing of Liszt's duets, including all Liszt's duet arrangements of other compositions, no matter how perfunctory, while Searle limits his duet catalogue to only three items.* However only a single one of these, the "Fest-Polonaise," is an authentic duet piece which was written originally for piano duet and exists in no other form. At present it can be found only as a part of the musical supplement to the Göllerich biography, issued in 1908, but it is a charming little thing, not at all difficult, which certainly deserves to be reprinted again. It is dated January 15, 1876 from the Villa d'Este, and was especially written for the marriage of the Princess Marie of Saxony. What a charming wedding gift, and how charming to imagine Liszt playing it with a friend on this oc-

* Various duet arrangements are, however, listed elsewhere in Searle's catalogue.

casion! The opening bars, marked *allegro pomposo,* will give some idea
of its festive character:

There is a more lyric second theme that soon appears in the key of E,
and after the reappearance of a few fragments of the opening theme,
we hear the second theme again, somewhat more majestically this
time in E flat. There is no development of any kind, and a brief coda
brings this amusing trifle to a brilliant conclusion. Liszt must have
tossed off this piece in an hour or two, but it is a charming thing all
the same, and there is no reason why it could not be returned to
circulation.

During Liszt's early days as a touring virtuoso, one of his favorite
pianistic battle horses was his own "Galop Chromatique," a sure-fire
stunner which he reserved as the last piece on the program, since it was
certain to bring the house down. Liszt made his own version of the
piece for piano duet (unfortunately not in print now, but available at
the Boston Music Library), filled with many new and delightful
touches, and in fact a finer work than the original solo version. It opens
humorously with a cheerful trumpet call, which turns out to be just a
semitone off key:

The continuation introduces a fresh and joyous motive, which is laid

out quite differently in the duet version, producing a new effect of
sonority:

Solo:

Duet:

After a scintillating middle section in A flat, the theme returns
slightly varied, *delicatamente* in the solo version, *scherzando* in the
duet version:

Solo:

Duet:

Certainly the original solo version is as complete and satisfactory as
can be imagined; yet Liszt contrives to turn up a few surprising appear-

ances of the theme in contrapuntal form in the duet arrangement. Here is one example:

Solo:

Duet:

At the very end, Liszt cuts four bars out of the duet version to make an even brighter and sharper ending. This delightful piece is a genuine contribution to the duet literature, which cries out for reprinting.

Another of Liszt's early concert pieces, the "Valse de Bravura" in B flat, also appeared in a contemporary duet version, and while Raabe doubts that Liszt made this transcription himself, there are enough new details in it to indicate Liszt's fine Italian hand, particularly in the *prestissimo* section toward the middle, which is almost entirely re-written. Perhaps some colleague may have drafted a duet arrangement to which Liszt added his own touches. After a brief introduction, the piece begins with this graceful and slightly Chopinesque theme:

There are old Chopinesque suggestions, or possibly allusions, during the course of this delightful dance, along with moments of pure Liszt, until the waltz breaks off, surprisingly enough, into a final section galop rhythm based on this variation of the opening theme:

While the duet version of this extended coda closely follows the outline of the solo version, Liszt—for it certainly must have been he—has taken splendid advantage of the added resonance possible to the duet medium, and has even added an extra bar to his closing passage as though to make more of it. Notice this remarkable distribution of the dominant seventh chord in the secondo part near the end, as the piece rushes along, *crescendo e molto stringendo,* to a smashing conclusion:

Certainly this precise sonority could have occurred only to Liszt; and to appreciate its originality you have only to compare it with any conventional treatment of the $V^7$ chord, such as this:

which would have sounded perfectly well, but which would have utterly missed the bite and pungency of Liszt's chord.

Like the "Galop Chromatique," this piece makes an excellent addition to the piano-duet literature, and with its slam-bang conclusion, it helps fill in a gap in the duet repertory, which is rather lacking in pieces that are effective on the concert stage as well as idiomatically written for the medium.

Another delightful work of Liszt, this dating from his later years, is the *Weihnachtsbaum* or "Christmas Tree" suite, which has only recently made its way back into print in its solo version. But Liszt himself is equally responsible for the duet as well as the solo version, and in a letter dated 1882 he writes, "Here is my modest Christmas Tree suite for both two hands and four hands." This is Liszt in a tender, intimate mood, where the garish lights of the concert stage are forgotten, and instead the warm glow of the fireside illuminates a happy family scene. The work is a set of twelve pieces suggested by varying aspects of Christmas—the singing of Christmas songs, the sound of Christmas bells and the joyful dances of the Christmas festivities.

The suite opens with a group of carols, the first "Ein Kleines Kinderlein," set very simply as though for children, followed by "O Heiliges Nacht" (not the familiar "Silent Night" but an older melody), this one set as though for an ethereal choir of angels. Then comes "In dulci jubilo," this time suggesting a delicate instrumental ensemble, with the *ostinato* figure of the secondo part given perhaps to an English horn. Then we hear the familiar "Adeste Fidelis" as though given forth by a brass choir. Now the caroling breaks off for a playful *scherzoso,* entitled "Lighting the Tree," filled with the atmosphere of childhood delight and expectancy, after which we hear the sound of Christmas bells in a brilliant "Carillon." By now the children are evidently ready for sleep, for the next piece is a gentle "Slumber Song," an exquisite piece in Liszt's tenderest mood. The older people then sing a charming old Provençal Christmas song, which fades away imperceptibly as we hear the "Evening Bells" of the following number. In *Jadis*—"Formerly"—the older people seem to think back to the days of their youth, seen through a nostalgic haze of distance. Like so many of the pieces of this set, it seems to disappear without our knowing it; and then the festivities end on a vigorous and cheerful note with two brilliant national dances, a Magyar "Ungarn" and a Polish mazurka.

Although Liszt made both the solo and duet versions himself, some of the pieces are clearly conceived as piano solos, while others work much better in the duet version. The opening Christmas songs, particularly, are piano solos which Liszt has made hardly any effort to really set for duet. For long stretches one player or the other simply goes on by himself while his partner has to sit silently and count measures. But the later pieces of the set are much finer in the duet version. Here for example are bars 37 to 45 of the "Slumber Song" in both versions, where the added melodic lines and ornamentation of the duet version make it much richer and more interesting:

Solo:

Duet:

It would be hard to say with certainty whether this piece was written first for duet and then simplified for the solo version, or written originally for solo and then developed and added to as Liszt transcribed it for duet. Probably the latter, for Liszt loved to rework his music, improving and retouching it as he went along. The brilliant closing section of the mazurka is also much more effective in the duet version, as a comparison of this brief passage in both versions will show:

Solo:

Duet:

This dance brings the collection to a rousing finish, and it is one of the few pieces in the set where Liszt allows himself anything like a conventional conclusion. Most of the others disappear in mid-air, like the "Chanson Provençal," with its closing six-four chords, or the "Scherzoso"

which outlines the closing chord in a single voice, pianissimo, or "Jadis" which ends questioningly outside the key. All the pieces of the set are rather short, and they are perhaps not all of quite equal merit: Some like the "Ungarn" with its quizzical ending, seem like a quick impression, a rough sketch, while others like the "Scherzoso" or the "Schlummerlied" are perfect little gems. But the work as a whole gives us a fascinating glimpse into a less familiar aspect of Liszt's style, and the later pieces at least make a very valuable addition to the duet repertory. It is interesting, by the way, that Liszt has altered the arrangement of the pieces in the two versions. In the solo version the five Christmas songs are all grouped together at the beginning, and Liszt allows the children to stay up a little later by putting the "Slumber Song" nearer the end, after "Carillon" and "Evening Bells." Curiously enough, the arrangement of the pieces seems equally logical and convincing either way. Certainly this work deserves to be better known, and in the duet version it might make an excellent concert piece, if a selection were made from the latter part of the collection that is more idiomatically written for duet.

In his catalogue of Liszt's compositions, Raabe includes a great number of duet versions of other compositions, such as the complete series of the symphonic poems, which Liszt himself arranged for piano duet as well as for two pianos, and many of the "Hungarian Rhapsodies," which are listed as being arranged from the orchestral transcriptions. There are also a number of duet arrangements of other solo compositions, and a number of works by other composers, nearly all of which are long out of print and virtually unobtainable.

However, we should make an exception for a series of duet arrangements that Liszt made of John Field's nocturnes for piano. Certainly this was a labor of love, for Liszt was a devoted admirer of Field's piano music, and particularly the nocturnes, for which he wrote a delightful critical study. Fortunately this Field arrangement is available at the Boston Music Library, and as a rarity you may perhaps wish to order it from them. It is quite different in concept from most of Liszt's arrangements, for there is no attempt whatever at the freedom and virtuosity that we usually find in Liszt's transcriptions. Instead Liszt has remained extremely faithful to his original, only highlighting it here and there with additional octaves, or delicately redistributing it so as to make it easier or more euphonious in the duet version. As a typical example of Liszt's approach, here is a brief excerpt from the opening of the nocturne in A flat, into which Liszt has introduced the favorite device of crossing hands between the partners:

Field:

Liszt:

A little later on Liszt has very delicately enhanced the iridescence of Field's pianistic tracery:

Field:

Liszt:

Liszt has chosen nine of Field's eighteen nocturnes to put in his duet version, including the familiar and beautiful one in B flat, and the longest and Liszt's favorite in A. None of them exceeds a moderate level of difficulty, and they are so perfectly adapted for their new medium that if we did not know the originals it would have been impossible to guess that they ever existed in any other form.

Field himself has left a little handful of pieces originally for piano duet, and while they are not quite as interesting as the best of his solo pieces, the nocturnes in particular, they are marked by his character-istic delicacy and refinement, and his imaginative feeling for the sonority of the piano, qualities that were to have such a profound influence on the piano style of Chopin and Liszt. A few of Field's duet pieces can be garnered in their original editions from various libraries: a charming and slightly Mozartean "Rondeau" in G is at the library of the Royal College of Music in London, while a number of other libraries have copies of the "Grande Valse" in A and a set of variations on a Russian air in A minor. Perhaps the best of the group is the Russian piece, which has quite an authentic Russian flavor. It will be remembered that Field spent much of his life in Russia, and Georgii has aptly pointed out the suggestion of balalaika effects in this piece which you can notice in the following brief excerpt. Here again there is crossing of hands between the partners; in this case with the *left* hand of the secondo player crossing to the upper part of the keyboard.

With the possible exception of the nocturnes, Field's compositions have become period pieces by now, but they are period pieces of con-siderable charm. Like Hummel, Field is interesting as a bridge between Mozart and Chopin, completely bypassing Beethoven.

Among the most curious contributions to the four-hand literature are the duet compositions of that extraordinary French master, Charles-Valentin Alkan. Alkan was highly regarded by some of the greatest among his contemporaries, Chopin and Liszt among them, and César Franck transcribed a number of his pieces for the organ and dedicated one of his own organ compositions to him. But Alkan is among those musical figures whose undeniable gifts and achievements have somehow failed to provide a place for them in the musical establishment, and whose posthumous fame has depended on the enthusiasm of occasional zealots.

Rowley lists three duet compositions of Alkan, a fantasy on *Don Juan*, opus 20, a set of three marches, opus 40, and a "Final" without opus number. Of these the three marches, opus 40, can be found at the Library of Congress, and even these are sufficient to provide some idea of Alkan's unique musical personality. Alkan was remarkably ingenious and inventive in his handling of the piano, and there are passages in these marches that demand a degree of virtuosity beyond anything normally found in the duet medium, while at the same time they are so clearly conceived as duet pieces that it is impossible to imagine them in any other form. Here are a few bars from the second march that will give you some inkling of Alkan's quite exceptional demands on his players. (Here again we have crossing of the hands, by the way.)

The American pianist, Raymond Lewenthal, has recently edited a volume of Alkan's solo compositions for Schirmer's, with data on Alkan's life and suggestions for interpreting his music. Together with these marches, it will help give you a picture of this nearly forgotten but quite extraordinary musician.

Another curiosity of the duet literature that you may wish to look up is Wagner's four-hand polonaise, opus 2, one of the very few instrumental compositions that he published in his own lifetime. Like his opus 1, a sonata for piano solo, it dates from his first musical studies in 1831, when he was eighteen, long before *Rienzi*, or even before his earliest and now forgotten operas, *Die Feen* and *Das Liebesverbot*. You may find it interesting less for its own sake than as an example of the almost incredible strides in Wagner's musical growth from a relatively unpromising beginning to *Tristan* and *Parsifal*. Even Mozart's first compositions written at the age of four are more Mozartean than this is Wagnerian. Largely influenced by Weber, the only visible hint of its composer is the instinctive confidence and authority of its musical speech.

Speaking of opera composers who have left their natural habitat of the theatre for the concert hall, you might note that Rossini left among the *Péchés de veillesse*—the name he gave to the trifles he threw off for his own amusement after he stopped writing operas—a few pieces for piano duet along with the songs and piano pieces that comprise the bulk of them. But these "sins," a few marches written for various occasions, have fewer redeeming qualities than most of the others; there is little of the true Rossinian sparkle and gaiety in them, and they are merely historical curiosities.

More interesting are a series of duet compositions, mostly "sonatas" in one movement, that the youthful Donizetti wrote during his early years of study in Bergamo. There are quite a number of them—seventeen in the catalogue of Weinstock—and although they are clearly student works, they still show an unexpected degree of charm and personality. Douglas Townsend has collected a group of them which are to be published by the firm of E. C. Kirbey, and while some are little more than Mozartean or Haydnesque echoes, although agreeable and well written all the same, they include such things as a delightful sonata in B flat in perpetual-motion style, sparkling and inventive in its sudden modulations. This brief excerpt will suggest something of the quality of this captivating trifle, which might make a perfect encore piece for a duet recital:

XII    *Grieg and Dvorak*

THERE was a time not too long ago when Grieg and Dvorak were considered more or less as equals—but in recent years Dvorak's star has been very much in ascendant, while Grieg has been relegated to the salon, or not far above it. It is true that Dvorak has the advantage of a far-greater productivity and development of style. Grieg's output is relatively slight, and apart from the *Peer Gynt* music, the piano concerto and a small handful of chamber music works, it consists almost entirely of individual songs and piano pieces.

But limited as Grieg's range is, the charm and freshness of his best work remains utterly unique, and his best work includes a small portfolio of four-hand compositions that are among the most beguiling things in the duet literature. Most familiar among them, no doubt, are the four "Norwegian Dances," opus 35, which have become almost hackneyed in the orchestral arrangement by Hans Sitt. But they are perfect examples of duet writing, and perhaps playing them in their four-hand version may help us capture something of their original freshness and color. All four are based on Norwegian folk dances and melodies, but as usual with Grieg, he has handled them in so uniquely personal a way that they have become entirely his own. The first begins with this quaint, wayward, march-like tune:

which soon builds up with remarkable impetus to a *fortissimo* of tremendous pianistic resonance, based on this augmentation of the opening motive in the lower part:

Suddenly a strangely poignant and mysterious middle section appears, in which Grieg mesmerizes us with his magical harmonic color. There would be no point in quoting this, for it must be heard in its entirety for its proper effect. After a return to the opening section, the piece ends wittily with this alternation of the two pianists:

The second dance is quaint and graceful. This time the girls seem to be dancing alone, but it is over before we know it. The third dance returns to the rustic, march-like character of the first. It is a perfect object lesson in how to make something of nothing, for the entire piece is based on this trifling little motive of the opening two measures:

In the middle section Grieg transmutes this into pure gold:

In this piece, by the way, be careful to observe the *moderato* of the tempo direction. It is by no means as fast as the first dance, and requires a certain deliberateness for the charm and humor of its main section to come through. The last piece, however, goes as fast as possible. Above one of Grieg's characteristic drone basses this tripping theme makes its appearance:

There is a slightly slower middle section which, however, never loses momentum, until at last the dance ends in a blazing *prestissimo*.

Grieg's two "Valses-Caprices," opus 37, are quite as fine as the "Norwegian Dances," but they have never been orchestrated, and are as unfamilar as the Norwegian Dances are hackneyed, so that we have the advantage of being able to come to them freshly. They are delightful examples of Grieg in his best vein; notice in the first, for example, the exquisite grace and lightness of touch of this cadence at the end of the main section:

In the middle section there is an amusing echo of the trio of the scherzo of the *Eroica* symphony—yet it sounds exactly like Grieg:

The second of two "Valses-Caprices" has appeared in a number of duet anthologies, and indeed its lilting and syncopated opening theme is quite delightful. The middle section consists of nothing more than the alternation of a series of shifting harmonies, first given to the secondo player in block chords, and then taken by both players in a shimmering figuration. Grieg lets us hear each new chord just long enough to savor its quality; it is as though a painter had laid a bright stroke of pure color on his canvas:

There may be a hint of the salon about these charming pieces, but in their perfect taste and freshness they are worlds removed from salon music.

Something of a special case in Grieg's output are the two symphonic pieces, opus 11, which are actually a duet arrangement of the middle movements of an early symphony. When Grieg, at the age of twenty, just out of the Leipzig Conservatory, was introduced to Neils Gade, that dean of Scandinavian composers asked what he had to show him. "Nothing," replied Grieg. "Well, go home and write me a symphony," Gade answered. Grieg did just that, turning out his first and only symphony in a remarkably short space of time. In later years Grieg was not satisfied with it and wrote on the title page, "Not to be performed," an injunction which has been observed to this day. But actually, we should very much like to hear it, and it is very possible that it might take a place with Bizet's symphony and the early symphonies of Schubert as a welcome youthful addition to the symphonic repertory.

Reversing the process, some of Grieg's duet pieces have become metamorphized into orchestral compositions, which have supplanted their original duet versions. Among them is Grieg's opus 11, originally published in 1867 as a fantasy for piano duet, and extended and orchestrated twenty years later to make the concert overture, "In Autumn." In the same category are the "Symphonic Dances," opus 64, which exist as duets, but are known now only in their orchestral form. They are later examples of the genre of the "Norwegian Dances," based like them on folk tunes, and filled with delicate charm, although perhaps lacking something of the strength and vigor of the earlier work.

Like Grieg, Dvorak arranged a number of his four-hand compositions for orchestra, the "Legends" and "Slavonic Dances" among them. Unlike Grieg, however, Dvorak is not primarily a composer for the piano, and his piano solo music rarely represents him at his best. But rather like Schubert, he found the piano duet medium particularly congenial, for it freed him from the limitations of the piano solo and served to stimulate his imagination.

Best known among his duet compositions are the wonderful "Slavonic Dances," which have become orchestral staples in Dvorak's own brilliant transcriptions, and which show him at the height of his power. There are two sets written eight years apart, and one hardly knows which one to admire more. If the second set is in some ways finer and more mature, the first is overflowing with a flavor of the Bohemian countryside that is absolutely irresistible. It opens with a burst of gaiety that in its freshness and vitality sets the tone for the entire set. This dance is based on the rhythm of the Bohemian *furiant,* marked by accents off the beat that give the three-quarter tempo a feeling of three-halves, and this rhythm gives the opening theme much of its individual character:

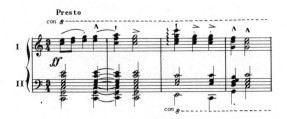

Brahms, who adored these dances, marveled that Dvorak was never at a loss for an idea. New themes and motifs flow ceaselessly from his pen, each one lovelier than the last.

The second dance in E minor begins in a mood of nostalgic sweetness, characteristic of the "Dumka," which soon breaks off into more vigorous rhythms. The third dance in D, which incidentally appears sixth in the orchestral version, is in a more rustic vein, almost humorous in its simplicity. The fourth dance again is in a different mood; it opens in a minuet tempo with a theme of such ravishing grace and simplicity that it must be quoted:

The fifth dance in A is as joyous and brilliant as the first, but now in a simpler and stronger 2/4 rhythm. With the sixth dance in A flat, the third of the orchestral set, we return again to a mellower mood. The Czech biographer of Dvorak, Otakar Sourek, calls it a polka, but it is a very idealized polka that takes on something of the character of one of Brahms' *allegretto grazioso* movements.

The seventh is more rustic again, close in feeling to the Czech folksongs. Although these dances are not arrangements of folksongs like Brahms' "Hungarian Dances," or to some degree, Grieg's "Norwegian Dances," Dvorak often uses a fragment of a folk melody as a germinating idea, and Dvorak's English biographer, John Clapham, quotes this melody as a possible source for it:

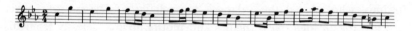

But how different it becomes in Dvorak's witty canonic treatment:

With the eighth and final dance of the set, Dvorak returns to the *furiant* rhythm of the opening. (*Furiant* means "swaggerer," incidentally, and both the first and last dances have exactly this quality.) Like the first, it opens in a burst of brilliance, but although it is in the minor, it moves even faster than the first and has a rather different feeling. Before it closes there is a little episode where Dvorak changes the minor mode to the major with a magic worthy of Schubert, and without any loss of the rustic Bohemian flavor so characteristic of the entire set.

Dvorak must have taken particular pleasure in composing these wonderful dances, and Sourek remarks that his pen raced across the paper, recording "only the bare melodic outline, almost without compositional notes." It is not surprising therefore to find that he returned to them later on to produce another set that is quite as wonderful as the first. In the eight years between the two sets his style had developed, and there is a quality of greater maturity about the second set, without however, any loss of verve or spontaneity. The second set opens as brilliantly as the first, but now the rhythm is more subtle, and the middle section of the first dance, marked *meno mosso,* shows a more refined treatment of the piano than we would have found earlier:

The following piece in E minor, in its mood of sadness and longing, is one of the loveliest of the set, and has made its appearance as an independent piece in many arrangements. The third number returns to a simpler rhythm and a more naive rustic flavor. The fourth has quite an individual harmonic flavor:

If you played the secondo part by itself you might very well take it for Debussy! The fifth is based on the following folksong—

which undergoes a remarkable metamorphosis in Dvorak's version:

The *Tempo di menuetto* of the sixth is a perfect foil for the succeeding *Presto,* which Dvorak must have written with the opening dance of the first set in his mind. It is one of the most brilliant of the entire series and would have made a stunning conclusion to the set. But Dvorak prefers to end on a quiet note, and the closing dance which follows is marked *lento grazioso, quasi tempo di valse.* What could be lovelier or more gracious than this theme?

Here as so often in Dvorak you must be particularly sensitive to the frequently indicated changes of tempo.

Although these lovely dances are the only duet compositions of Dvorak that have become generally familiar, the ten "Legends" of opus 59, written midway between the two sets, are fully on a level with them. If they have not made their way equally with the public, it may

be that this suite is too long to play as a single work, and perhaps also
that there is too great a variety of style within it to make a consistent
whole. The first three pieces are delightful examples of Dvorak's
Bohemian style, and the third in particular might have come right out
of the "Slavonic Dances." The fourth is rather different; more serious,
and even solemn, with its trumpet calls and chorale passages, its rushing scales and martial strains, it might be a miniature symphonic poem
on some historical or religious theme. But its frequent changes of mood
and tempo require very careful playing to hold it together. The fifth
piece that follows also suggests a religious connotation with its contrapuntal texture and its organ-like passages, and Sourek finds in it the
"delicately tinted portrait of a female saint."

The "Legends" are published in two books of five pieces each, and
if you consider the last five pieces of the second book as a group in
itself, then it can make a consistent work which might be performed
as a whole. The first piece of the second book in C sharp minor is in a
wonderfully broad and expansive vein, with something almost symphonic about it. From the very first notes you can sense that Dvorak
is at the top of his form:

Near the beginning Dvorak introduces a figure in quickly repeated
triplet notes, that seems to sustain the momentum throughout, even
during a relatively tranquil slower middle section in the major. Particularly poetic is the ending, that seems almost to vanish before our
eyes:

The following piece is an *allegretto grazioso* in A major based on a curiously syncopated rhythm, which fully maintains the poetic level of the first. Notice in this passage from the middle section with what a perfect touch Dvorak has mastered the chamber music quality of the duet medium:

Next comes a quiet, pastorale-like movement in F, fully as lovely as what has gone before. One is tempted to quote from it, except that it would be too hard to know where to stop. The last two legends are final evocations of Dvorak's Bohemian countryside, dance-like still, but in a quieter and more lyrical vein.

These legends are among the finest things in the duet literature—works that forever disclose new beauties. One can only echo Brahms, who wrote to the publisher Simrock shortly after they appeared: "Tell Dvorak how the Legends continue to charm me. One envies the fresh, cheerful and rich resourcefulness of the man."

Dvorak composed one more extended work for piano duet, a suite entitled "From the Bohemian Forest," opus 68, especially at the request of the publisher Simrock, who wanted to follow up the success of the "Legends" and the "Slavonic Dances." It consists of a set of six pieces suggested by various aspects of the southwestern corner of Bohemia where Dvorak spent his summers: The Spinning Room, The Black Lake, Walpurgis Night, Silent Woods, In Wait, and In Stormy Times. In spite of many fine touches, the suite does not come off as successfully as Dvorak's other duet works. Perhaps Dvorak's heart was not fully in it, for it does have a little the air of a commissioned work. Those Bohemian girls in the spinning room are a little too self-consciously charming, and although the witches at the Walpurgis Night festival go through all the motions they do not really frighten us. And in the last movement the wind howls and the trees shake, but we seem to see it from behind the lace curtains of a warm and cozy cottage.

Perhaps the best number of the set is "Silent Woods" which Dvorak liked well enough to arrange for cello and piano, and later for small orchestra. Somehow for once in the work Dvorak succeeds in becoming involved, and it has some beautiful moments of a somber, almost Brahmsian cast:

Dvorak, like so many extremely prolific composers, is not always consistently at the same level. But at his best he is beyond praise, and his best duets rank him with Mozart, with Schubert and with Brahms among the great masters of the medium.

XIII 🐝 *The Russians*

Iɴ ᴄᴏɴᴛʀᴀsᴛ to the great line of German masters, who were almost all pianists and composers for the piano, the Russian composers were generally speaking more absorbed in the orchestra and in problems of instrumental color. Even Tschaikowsky, with his splendid piano concerto in B flat minor, has left nothing for piano solo that has remained in the repertoire, and the nationalist school of the Russian Five was even more exclusively preoccupied with the orchestra and with the opera house. It is not surprising, therefore, to find that with their rather limited interest in the piano they left relatively little for piano duet. Yet all the same, if we search out the duet compositions of the Russian composers we will find among them not a few things of genuine value and interest.

Tschaikowsky, for example, has left only one work for piano duet, and that only a series of arrangements of Russian folksongs, yet it is a work to cherish, and perhaps the ideal means of introducing a talented youngster to the piano duet. Tschaikowsky has arranged these melodies in the simplest possible way, with at least one of the parts, and sometimes both, easy enough for beginners to handle without difficulty. Usually he merely repeats the melody twice, with a slight variation the second time, perhaps a new touch of harmony, or a new contrapuntal part. But it is remarkable how in just a line or two these harmonizations catch the very essence of a Russian style.

Tschaikowsky was steeped in Russian folk music from his earliest childhood, and he anticipated many later folk song scholars in taking every opportunity to copy down the folk songs he heard on his travel through the Russian countryside. Sometimes these lovely melodies have a suggestion of modal quality about them which Tschaikowsky invariably seizes on with a perfect and inevitable rightness. Sometimes they end on an unexpected note of the scale or the harmony, which Tschaikowsky makes no attempt to conventionalize. Frequently Tschaikowsky has notated subtle rhythmical variations from one measure to the next, as in this lovely melody, which perhaps you may recognize as the *andante cantabile* of the first quartet:

Here is a typical setting of one of the stronger, more diatonic melodies, *Nye tesan terem,* "The Attic." Although it is in a simple two quarter time, the phrases are in five bars throughout:

Tschaikowsky was more than usually obliging in this case to give us a tonic chord to end with, for often enough he is likely to leave us hanging in mid-air harmonically, as in this ending to *U vorot,* "At the Gate":

But after you have played this ending a few times, you will realize that it is the only possible one.

It would be hard to recommend these little arrangements too highly. Not only are they easy enough for students to master, but their attention will be kept alert by the numerous rhythmic and harmonic surprises. And playing through them is something like taking a tour of Russian musical history, for scattered among them you will recognize melodies that Tschaikowsky used in his symphonic and chamber music, Rimsky-Korsakoff in his operas and Stravinsky in his ballets. Fortunately these delightful folk song arrangements are available in a variety of editions, among which the Peters edition and the International edition identify many of the tunes used in other compositions, and the Peters edition, although it selects only thirty-six out of the complete fifty songs, offers an excellent introductory article by the editor, Kurt Herrmann.

Before going ahead, let us take a moment to glance at an earlier composer, Michael Glinka (1804–1857) who is idolized by Russian musicians as "the father of Russian music," and whose two major operas, *A Life for the Czar* and *Russlan and Ludmilla* are still in the repertory of Russian opera houses. Glinka is unusual among Russian composers in having left a sizable body of duet music, which has been reissued in one volume by the Russian Publishing House, and is available in the United States through the Leeds Music Company. In spite of the exalted status that Glinka is accorded in his own country, he is often likely to strike Westerners as an inspired amateur, and while these duet compositions all have delightful moments, none of them is quite strong enough to take a place in the permanent duet repertoire. The longest piece in the collection is a "Capriccio on Russian Themes," which seems like a kind of pianistic sketch for his better known and more successful orchestral fantasy on two Russian folksongs, the captivating, "Kamarinskaya." But whereas the orchestral work is compact and masterly in every note, the piano duet alternates delightful passages with sections that seem to flounder about a little, particularly a fugato toward the end that leads to an interminable coda.

Perhaps the most successful of Glinka's duet pieces is a polka in B flat, whose charm can be gauged from the infectious folk gaiety of its opening theme:

This piece is developed with sparkling variations and interludes of new material, one of which combines with the main theme at the end to bring the work to a witty close. In addition to these two longer works, the Glinka duet collection also contains two "Trots de Cavalerie," spirited little numbers in a galop rhythm, and an "Impromptu en Galop" based on the barcarolle from Donizetti's *Elisir d'Amore*.

Among the composers of the great nationalistic school of the Russian Five, only the eldest and mentor of them all, Balakirev (1836–1910) displayed any particular interest in the piano, and if he is remembered today as a composer, it is solely by virtue of his brilliant pianistic concert piece, "Islamey." Balakirev's career as a composer is unusual in that he produced much of his best work at an early age, and then after a long period of silence returned to composition again only at the end of his life. Balakirev left two works for piano duet, both dating from his last years, a suite written in 1908, and a set of thirty arrangements of Russian folk songs, dating from 1898. The suite is an interesting work in three movements, a fine polonaise, a charming "Chansonette sans Paroles," and an extended and inventive scherzo. Unfortunately it is no longer in print, but there is a copy in the Music Division of the Library of Congress, and piano duet players who are interested in finding new material might do very well to look into it. Balakirev's thirty folk song arrangements were first written for voice and piano, and then arranged by Balakirev for piano duet. Naturally, they can hardly avoid comparison with Tschaikowsky's similar set of fifty. Balakirev's arrangements are generally a little longer than Tschaikowsky's and more sophisticated in pianistic treatment, but although they are charming and interesting, they lack the power and directness of Tschaikowsky's settings, and do not rank in the same class with them.

Balakirev's pupil and disciple, Moussorgsky, has left one work for piano duet, written during his student years, an allegro in symphonic style, obviously intended as a sketch for a symphony. This piece very much pleased his teacher Balakirev and his fellow-pupil Rimsky-Korsakoff, and after having remained in manuscript for many years was printed in 1939 in the complete Russian edition of Moussorgsky's works, and reprinted in Erno Balogh's anthology of *Eighteen Original Piano Duets,* published by Schirmer's in 1943. In spite of obvious

reminiscences of Schubert's great C major symphony (which Moussorgsky and his friends must have played as a piano duet, for it was their
custom to acquaint themselves with the standard symphonic repertory
in this manner), the work already shows traces of Moussorgsky's gifts,
and just before the end, a touch of genuine personality in these
Moussorgskian progressions:

Appended to this work is a scherzo in C minor which Moussorgsky
arranged for duet from an earlier scherzo in C sharp minor for piano
solo. Perhaps Moussorgsky may have been thinking of extending this
work into a full length symphonic form, but all we possess are these
two opening movements, which are, however, of interest as youthful
works of a fascinating musical personality.

Moussorgsky's friend and fellow pupil with Balakirev, Borodin, left
only two small compositions for piano duet, a tarantella and polka.
Neither is in print, but the tarantella is available at the Library of
Congress, and like Moussorgsky's allegro, has the appearance of being
a student work—well written, effective, not without charm, and like the
Moussorgsky piece, filled with reminiscences, in this case of the finale
to Mendelssohn's *Italian Symphony*.

César Cui, the least known of the Russian Five, has written a set
of "Ten Pieces for Five Fingers," which if not a major work, is still a
welcome addition to the long series of five finger duet pieces for student and teacher. This too is out of print, but to judge by the first five
in the set in the New York Music Library, well deserves to be reprinted,
for they are varied, skillfully written, and quite charming in a Russian
manner.

Rimsky-Korsakoff is the only one of the Russian Five who has left
nothing specifically for piano duet, but he does have a very special

place of his own in the history of piano ensemble music, for it was he who instigated that almost unknown but quite extraordinary tour de force, the "Paraphrases on Chopsticks." This work was written jointly by three members of "The Five," Rimsky-Korsakoff, Borodin, and César Cui, joined by a younger and very talented composer friend, Anatol Liadov, and it consists, as the title page points out, of "twenty-four variations and fifteen little pieces for piano on the following theme

dedicated to the little pianists capable of executing it with one finger of each hand." Against this version of chopsticks, repeated over and over again in the treble, the four collaborators have concocted an amazing collection of pieces in an almost endless variety of styles.

Rimsky-Korsakoff in his biography, *My Musical Life* describes the origin of his work. "Some years before," he writes, "Borodin, in fun, had composed a most charming and odd polka on the following motive of chopsticks. Repeated over and over again, this motive was intended, so to speak, for one unable to play the piano, while the accompaniment called for a real pianist. As I recall it, I was the first to conceive the idea of writing, jointly with Borodin, a series of variations and pieces on this theme, constant and unchanging. Later I induced Cui and Liadov to join in this work."

The contents include, after the opening set of twenty-four variations, a polka, funeral march, waltz, berceuse, galop, gigue, fughetta on the name of BACH—but why go on; if you possibly can, go out and get the work yourself, and fortunately it is available as republished by the firm of Boosey and Hawkes. These pieces are not only ingenious but charming and musical as well, and one can only surmise that their neglect is due to the unconventionality of the idea, added to the fact that it would be by no means easy to find a child, or an adult either, who could repeat that little chopsticks motive over and over again without losing his patience or his sanity.

Sometimes the collaborators indulge in recherché harmonic experiments, as in this excerpt from the opening variations by Rimsky-Korsakoff:

More often the ingenuity is rhythmic, as in this little mazurka by Borodin:

Here is another tricky rhythmical nut to crack, in the waltz by César Cui:

On the basis of this brilliant waltz, perhaps Cui is a better composer than we have been accustomed to consider him.

Rimsky-Korsakoff tells us how one day he played a little fughetta complete with stretto on the name BACH to Cui, who was not overly impressed with it. "Then I asked him to play chopsticks," Rimsky-Korsakoff goes on, "while I struck up the fugue":

"Cui could not get over his amazement," Rimsky-Korsakoff adds.

One of the pieces, the "Carillon" by Rimsky-Korsakoff, is written for piano duet in addition to the two hands playing chopsticks in the treble, and it too poses a few unexpectedly tricky rhythmical problems. Liszt was very much taken with this collection of paraphrases on chopsticks, and even contributed a little *morceau* for piano solo suggested by the chopsticks motive, which was reprinted in facsimile in later editions. Liszt's pupil, Siloti, tells us that he liked to play the "Paraphrases" with his pupils after the lessons were over.

> One of us had to play the variations while he played the 'theme,' giving himself up to the enjoyment of each number. He very much liked tripping up any young musician who did not know the work with the "Carillon." Showing him the two apparently simple pages, he would say with a touch of malice, "Can you play this at sight?"

Needless to say, the unsuspecting pianist invariably accepted, and invariably lost his way, much to Liszt's delight!

Liadov's contributions to the "Paraphrases" are charming too. But Liadov, although extremely talented, was notoriously lazy, and his small list of published works includes nothing for duet apart from the four pieces he wrote for this collection. Among the numerous other gifted, if minor, Russian composers of this era, we should not overlook Anton Arensky, whose piano music and chamber compositions were once popular in Russia and indeed all over Europe, and whose masterly and polished technique as well as winning sentiment raises them well above the level of salon music. Arensky has left a charming set of children's pieces opus 34 for piano duet which are valuable additions to the duet repertoire at an intermediate level of difficulty. Each of the pieces is suggested by some particular conceit—a fugato on a popular tune, a piece in 5/4 time in the Phyrigian mode, or this clever berceuse, in which the secondo player is limited throughout to the open strings of the cello, with perfectly charming effect:

Andante sostenuto

Attractive as it is, Arensky's music seems to be gradually disappearing from the repertoire. But curiously enough, the music of his pupil, Rachmaninoff, which many musicians were ready to dismiss out of hand during his lifetime, seems to gain added stature with the passing years. Rachmaninoff was very much a composer for the piano—not exclusively, as his hauntingly beautiful *Second Symphony* will testify —but a large portion of his output is for piano alone or in combination with other instruments. His major effort in ensemble music for the piano is represented in two splendid suites for two pianos, which are among the major productions of his earlier years. But he did leave one work for piano duet, a set of six pieces, opus 11, dating from 1895 which, if not quite as serious or ambitious a work as the suites for two pianos, is nevertheless a valuable addition to the duet repertory.

The first piece of the set is a barcarolle that opens with deceptive simplicity in a delicate chamber music style, but builds up by almost imperceptible steps until in the middle section it reaches a climax of remarkable power, in which the secondo player thunders out sonorous chords against a cascade of pianistic figurations in the upper part. Little by little they subside as the opening theme returns in the lower part, until at last they die out on a *pianissimo* level almost as delicate as the opening. This piece is filled with Rachmaninoff's personal, almost hypnotic poignancy of harmonic color, and is executed on a scale and with a power that puts it quite beyond the level of Arensky's charming but slighter things. The following number is a scintillating scherzo, full of pianistic surprises, with not a dull moment from the first note to the last.

If the first two pieces are the finest of the set, the rest of the suite is also interesting and characteristic, well worth knowing. The third piece begins with a little Russian melody that might almost have come out of one of Tschaikowsky's folk song settings, but here it is extended and developed in a series of masterly variations. Rachmaninoff is one of those composers whose style is almost immediately recognizable, but the little waltz which is the fourth piece of the set is one of those rare cases in Rachmaninoff's work where we might hardly guess the composer if we didn't know to begin with. The opening has something of a French manner about it, and one might be inclined to wonder if it were Fauré, until a few unexpected dissonances suggest the possibility of Poulenc. The middle section, with its insistently repeated chords in the lower part would still hardly call Rachmaninoff to mind. Perhaps Sibelius might be a more likely possibility. This piece as a whole shows us an unexpected side of Rachmaninoff's musical personality, more experimental harmonically than we expect from him.

With the fifth piece, the romance, there is no doubt about the composer—it is Rachmaninoff from the first bar—although still more experimental harmonically than usual. As the last piece opens, we immediately recognize the famous Russian melody that Beethoven has used in the Rasomoffsky quartets and Moussorgsky in *Boris Goudonoff.* Instead of building variations on his melody, as in the third piece, Rachmaninoff here constructs a free fantasy on motives taken from it, developed in a variety of keys and tempos, and in a very free pianistic style. At the change to 6/4 time toward the end, be sure to count each of the six beats in the measure, even in this quick tempo, or else you may be thrown rhythmically, for the lower part actually begins in 3/2 time with three main beats to a measure. Later on Rachmaninoff does spell out the rhythm in terms of 6/4 time. This finale ends in a blaze of pianistic fireworks, bringing this unique contribution to the piano duet literature to a brilliant close.

Generally speaking, contemporary composers have not been too interested in the piano duet, and among Soviet composers, neither Prokofieff nor Shostakovitch have displayed any particular interest in piano ensemble music, even though Prokofieff's remarkable series of piano solo pieces and sonatas have made him outstanding among contemporary composers for the piano.

Stravinsky, however, is something of an exception in this respect, for he has written a good deal for two pianos, and in *"Les Noces,"* has even doubled that number to four. Stravinsky's piano duet music is on a modest scale, but is characteristic and interesting all the same. Fortunately, Stravinsky's two works for piano duet have been reprinted a number of times, and you can find both of them complete in the Schirmer's anthology of *Eighteen Original Piano Duets* edited by Erno Balogh. Both these works are in the tradition of educational piano duet music, calling for an easier part for the student and a more difficult one for the teacher, but even here Stravinsky has done things his own way, and both the two sets are full of surprises.

The first of the two sets, consisting of three pieces written in 1915, has a complicated upper part for the teacher, while the student has to content himself with these three *bassi ostinati:*

These three absurdly simple basses actually create problems from a practical point of view, and in the opening march only a quite exceptional student could be expected to kep his footing against the changing time signatures and the wry dissonances in the upper part. In the following two pieces, a kind of "wrong-note" valse, and a quite zany galop, things are a little easier, with a touch of variety in the left hand part, and since there are no changes in the time signature, the student can at least keep going without having to count. But the upper parts are rather difficult, and the teacher may have to do quite a bit of practicing himself to handle them. All three of these pieces are marked by Stravinsky's dryest and most subtle musical wit, of which perhaps this brief excerpt from the galop may give you an idea:

Almost as though to atone for having given the student such a hard time in the first set of pieces, the five pieces of the second set, dating

from 1917, in which the primo part is easier, offer a much more attractive and grateful part for the student player. The opening *andante*
of the second set is quite simple enough to be played by two beginners,
and this excerpt will offer some idea of its grave and rather austere
beauty:

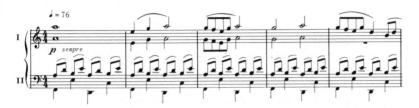

The following piece, "Espagnola" has a very difficult left hand part
for the teacher, and the upper part too will require very careful count-
ing and concentration, if the pupil is not to get lost. The remaining
three pieces of the set are somewhat more accessible, and the finale,
another galop, starts off in this mood of infectious gaiety:

Actually, none of these pieces, with the sole exception of the *andante*
of the second set, is really practical for children. But for older students with some degree of musical maturity, they are an excellent introduction to Stravinsky, and indeed, to modern music in general.

# XIV ⁂ *The French*
## *Bizet, Fauré,*
## *Ravel, Debussy*

The French, like the Russians, were rather late in coming to the piano duet, but when they did, they took it up with an enthusiasm that equaled and perhaps surpassed that of any other nation. Alec Rowley, in his excellent handbook of the piano duet—actually a listing of music in print, with occasional brief comments—has a separate section for French composers that is quite remarkable in its profusion and variety. Nearly every French composer, great or small, seems to have made some contribution to the piano duet, and as though to make up for their late start, they continued to produce masterpieces for it up to the time of the First World War. Thus, while the earlier period of the piano duet is centered in the Vienna of Mozart and Schubert, the later history of the piano duet reaches its high point in the Paris of Debussy and Ravel.

However, none of the French composers left quite as substantial a body of work for this medium as Schubert or Brahms or Dvorak. The history of the piano duet in France is outlined rather in a series of isolated masterpieces, which begins in 1865 with the appearance of Bizet's "Jeux d'Enfants."

For the general public, Bizet is the composer of *Carmen,* perhaps the best-loved opera ever written. Music lovers know him as well for the lovely incidental music to "L'Arlésienne," one of the treasures of the repertory for small orchestra. But in the "Jeux d'Enfants," piano duettists have a third work to place alongside these two. It is one of the most delightful of duet works and stands first in line of the series of children's suites for piano duet, for which the French composers were to show a special partiality.

Although "Jeux d'Enfants" antedates "L'Arlésienne" by two years and *Carmen* by five, it already shows Bizet's gifts at their richest and most characteristic. Like Schumann's "Scenes from Childhood" it is a suite about children rather than for children, for although it contains a few pieces of only moderate difficulty, the technical level of skill it demands is generally quite advanced. Each of the twelve pieces in the set depicts some aspect of children's playtime—the seesaw, spinning a top, riding on the merry-go-round, blowing soap bubbles and so on. Although Bizet thought of himself as an opera composer, and once complained to Saint-Saëns, "You can compose anytime, but I must depend on a good libretto," yet in this suite he found an idea that was a perfect springboard for his truly remarkable gift of musical illustration.

Notice in "La Toupie" for example, how cleverly Bizet suggests a top losing its momentum, coming to a pause, and then reeling away crazily before falling:

And in "Blindman's Buff" you can almost see the little blindfolded child stumble as he reaches and seizes on his victim:

There are moments of tender sentiment in "Little Husband, Little Wife" and of wistful innocence in "La Poupée" that clearly show the same hand that was later to create the more lyrical moments of Micaela's part in *Carmen*. But the entire suite is a brilliant and adorable work, that remains one of the cornerstones of the piano duet repertory. Bizet himself orchestrated five numbers of the suite, and the work has more than once been used as a musical setting for ballet.

Somehow the French composers have been particularly drawn to this genre of pieces for children, or rather, pieces describing childhood, and another of the loveliest examples of this type is Fauré's piano duet suite, "Dolly," opus 56. Fauré is a composer who has not gained quite the recognition outside of his own native country that he deserves, but the French rank him as one of their supreme masters, and there is an exquisite delicacy and grace about Fauré's music at its best that is inimitable. You will find it in his incidental music to Maeterlinck's play "Pelléas and Mélisande," in certain moments in his songs and chamber music, and in this lovely set of piano duet pieces as well.

The "Dolly" of the title refers to the young daughter of Fauré's friend, the soprano Emma Bardac, for whom he wrote his song cycle, "La Bonne Chanson" and who was later to become Debussy's second wife. These pieces are not illustrative in quite the same sense as Bizet's "Jeux d'Enfants"; rather they illuminate some typical mood or scene of childhood. The opening berceuse for example suggests a moment of childhood peace and quietness, perhaps a little girl rocking

Gabriel Fauré.
*The Bettmann Archive*

her doll to sleep; but simple as it is, it is a perfect introduction to Fauré's music.

The second piece of the set, "Miaou" is more lively, and following the suggestion of the title, Fauré's biographer, Emile Vuillermoz sees in it "the capricious bounds of the favorite family cat, its quick turns, its zigzag starts, its sudden cajolery, after which, wearied by its tumultuous agitation, it at last rests in the lap of its little mistress." This description seems perfectly to illustrate the elusive whimsy of this delightful piece—but the pianist Marguerite Long, on the basis of her close friendship with Fauré, asserts instead that the title of the piece is a nickname for Dolly's brother Raoul, of whom this piece is, instead, a musical portrait! In either case, it is an utterly delightful thing, and incidentally, not at all easy, with its cross rhythms and un-expected accents in the lower part.

The middle section is based on a little leaping phrase that modu-lates to a different cadence on each appearance, and these unexpected and yet inevitable modulations each seem to capture something of Fauré's very personal and intimate charm:

How can you explain the magic of such a passage as that? It is as irresistible as the smile of a child.

The "Jardin de Dolly" which follows is equally lovely—a brief stroll with Dolly through her flower garden. When the melody ap-pears softly in the tenor voice of the secondo part, the arpeggios of the upper part must be just barely touched:

The mood is lighter in the next piece, "Kitty-Valse." Vuillermoz sees in it "all the grace and lightness of a little girl's dance, in which we already sense the feminine seduction of the woman she is to be tomorrow," a perfectly apt description of the piece; but Marguerite Long tells us that it depicts rather "the whirling turns of a favorite dog!" Well, it really doesn't matter; the piece is charming in any case, even if slightly more frivolous than the rest of the work.

The following movement, "Tendresse" is the most touching piece of the set, but touching with a subtlety than can easily escape you unless you are attuned to the delicacy of Fauré's style. Be sure to follow the directions of loud and soft precisely as Fauré has indicated them; the crescendo to a *fortissimo* at the end of the first section lifts it to an intense and powerful emotional level, but you must sustain it for exactly the three measures that Fauré has indicated, and then diminuendo in just one measure from *fortissimo* to *piano*. The middle section is a canon between the lower and the upper voices, of so articulate a quality that it might almost be a conversation between mother and child. On the return to the first part there are no more words, only feelings of purest tenderness.

The finale, a "Pas Espagnol" is in a lighter mood. Here again we might very well follow Vuillermoz' cue, who finds in it not really a Spanish dance, but rather a little girl who has thrown her mother's Spanish shawl around her, and takes the stage for a moment. If you have learned to play and love this suite, perhaps it may serve as an introduction to the beauty of Fauré's musical language. For many people Fauré is an acquired musical taste; he seduces rather than overwhelms you, but once you have learned to appreciate him he will be a precious and irreplaceable part of your musical world.

Fauré's pupil Ravel has also written a piano duet suite inspired by childhood, but in many respects a very different one from Fauré's. It is less personal and more abstract in mood, being intended not as remembrances of childhood, but as a musical illustration for some of the lovely fairy tales for children found in various French collections. Perhaps something of the success of these pieces may be attributed to Ravel's particular sympathy for children; he was a tiny man himself, hardly bigger than they, and often when visiting friends he would disappear for long periods of time, only to be discovered playing with the children as one of them. Ravel has written of this suite, "My intention of awakening the poetry of childhood in these pieces naturally led me to simplify my style and thin out my writing." This suite was written for Jean and Mimi Godebski, children of friends of his, and was intended to be easy enough for them to play. At its first public performance in Paris in 1910, it was actually performed by two little girls, aged seven and eight.

The first piece of the set, "The Pavane of the Sleeping Beauty" seems to conjure up for us the magical forest in which the princess and all her courtiers and servants have been enchanted into a hundred years sleep. It is only five short phrases in length, and offers no technical problems, even for beginners. You must only be careful to maintain the slow and measured tempo that Ravel has indicated, and not speed up even by a hair's breadth. But when this piece is well played, it never fails to cast its spell. We can almost feel the cobwebs and see the strange light of the supernatural forest. Once when this piece was played for a group of non-musicians who were asked to tell what thoughts it aroused, one girl imagined the stars in their courses, and then, as an afterthought, suggested the strange feeling that might be experienced in trying to return to normal life after a long period of mental illness. When the pictures of the lunar landscape were first transmitted back to earth, no musical background was offered; but if there had been one, nothing could have been more perfect than this curiously evocative piece.

The next number is hardly more difficult than the first, and again it attains the most poetical effects with the simplest means. It tells the story of "Le Petit Poucet," the little boy who wandered into the woods, and left bread crumbs as he walked so that he could find his way back, only to discover when he returned that the birds had eaten them all. Notice with what delicate strokes Ravel suggests the call of the birds.

Certainly this moment must rank, along with the famous passage at the end of the slow movement of Beethoven's *Pastoral Symphony*, among the classic examples of the representation of bird calls in music.

The third piece, "Laideronette" brings us to the Orient as we hear the story of the little Chinese Empress of the Pagodas, whose tiny magical pagodas danced and sang for her while playing tiny instruments made out of nut shells. This piece is a veritable tour de force. for the black keys, based entirely on the pentatonic scale of F sharp; and for the first time in the suite, it is not at all easy.

The next piece, one of the most charming and touching of the set, tells us the story of Beauty and the Beast. At first we hear the conversation of Beauty, all innocence and grace, as though to translate into music the first line of the conversation printed above the score: "When I think of your good heart, you don't seem so ugly":

And then the answer of the Beast: "Yes, lady, I have a good heart, but I am a monster":

Notice how delicately Ravel indicates the involuntary shuddering of the Beauty in the fourths of the upper part. But as we all know, the story ends happily as the Beauty promises to marry the monster, and finds that he has turned into a handsome prince. Now the Beast's motive is transposed into the highest register of the piano, and the waltz rhythm of the lower part gives way to sustained chords:

The entire suite ends with a musical portrayal of "Le Jardin Fée-rique", the magic garden, in a slow sarabande tempo, as though to balance the pavane of the opening, and almost entirely on the white keys, as though to balance the black key study of the Chinese Pagodas.

This suite is very well known in its orchestral version, and has also been made into a ballet, for which Ravel has provided a little additional music. Ravel has added a new dimension to this work in his marvelous orchestration, and it would be ungrateful to begrudge this work to a larger musical public; but all the same, piano duettists may be excused for feeling a special affection for this work in its original version.

Debussy too has made an offering to childhood in his delightful "Children's Corner" suite, but this of course is a work for piano solo. However, in his early "Petite Suite" for piano duet, one of the very earliest things we know him by, Debussy has left a piano duet work of a charm and intimacy that has a close affinity with the children's piano duet suites of Bizet, Fauré and Ravel. This work has become extremely popular with light orchestras in the arrangement by Henri Busser, and like many of Debussy's early things, it is filled with a grace and charm that are surprisingly close to the style of the salon. But if the echoes of Massenet and Delibes are quite apparent in this work, there are also hints of the Debussy that was to come, as in this little whole tone passage from the first of its four movements, "En Bateau":

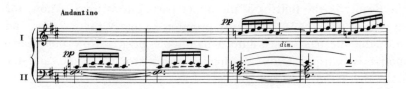

Although this charming piece is marked *andantino*, it must be taken at a flowing two counts to the measure, if the melody is to sing out easily and naturally.

The following "Cortège" is as graceful and winning as can be imagined. Note Debussy's delicacy of touch in the slight variations of the secondo part on each successive reappearance of the theme, as the upper part remains unchanged throughout:

The minuet that follows recalls the eighteenth century as seen through a haze of nineteenth-century sentiment:

A brilliant little finale entitled "Ballet" brings this delightful and effective suite to a close.

If the "Petite Suite" of 1889 marks the beginning of Debussy's earliest style, then his other suite for piano duet, the "Epigraphes Antiques" of 1915 brings us the maturest style of his last period. Debussy's three periods are as clearly defined as Beethoven's, and the distance he has traveled is equally far. It would have been as impossible to imagine the rarefied subtlety of the "Epigraphes Antiques" from the Massenet-like sentiment of the "Petite Suite" as it would have been to predicate Beethoven's last quartets from the minuet in G, if we didn't have the intervening steps as evidence. As with Beethoven, Debussy's last works are on a level of subtlety and abstraction that have prevented them from becoming as widely popular as the works of the early and middle periods; but to specialists and professionals, these late works have a special and unique fascination.

Debussy's biographers have told us that the "Epigraphes Antiques" are derived from sketches dating from Debussy's middle years; but perhaps that may be almost as irrelevant as the fact that a passage of Beethoven's quartet, opus 132, is taken from one of Beethoven's boyhood works. The "Epigraphes Antiques" are in essence of Debussy's latest period, and rank among the most individual and poetic of the works of his last years. Only perhaps in the first piece of the set, "Pour invoquer Pan, dieu du vent d'été," can we clearly recognize an affinity with his earlier style, and indeed, such a passage as this might almost not have seemed out of place in the "Petite Suite":

But with the second piece of the set, "Pour un tombeau sans nom," we are already in Debussy's maturest manner, and by way of contrast, such a passage as this would not seem out of place in a work of Stravinsky or Bartok:

To correctly interpret these subtle chords, you must remember that Debussy is said to have played the piano himself in such a way as to make his listeners forget that it had hammers. At the end of the piece, these delicate dissonances form the background to a kind of whispered sob in the upper part that brings the composition to a close.

The third piece, "Pour que la nuit soit propice," is filled with passages such as the following that are equally subtle, rhythmically and harmonically:

The next two pieces, "Pour la danseuse aux crotales" (for the snake dancer) and "Pour l'Egyptienne," are more outwardly picturesque, and one ventures to guess, probably derived more directly from their original models of 1899, first intended as incidental background to a work of Pierre Louys.

The closing piece, "Pour remercier la pluie du matin," is the last of Debussy's pianistic representations of the rain, which he has drawn with such imagination and variety in so many of the earlier piano pieces and songs. The upper part indicates a delicate and monotonous patter of rain, while intertwined with it, above and below, the secondo part weaves a delicate and varied contrapuntal pattern:

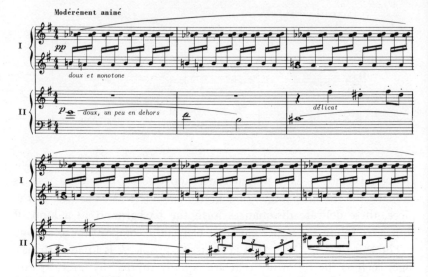

A brief momentary return to the opening of the first piece closes this unique work, one of the most subtle and poetic in the entire range of the duet literature.

Debussy has left one other work for piano duet, which surprisingly enough, is almost unknown, although it is an early work in his most delightful and accessible manner. Dating from 1891, two years after the "Petite Suite," it was written on commission from a Scottish general who wished to have a musical setting of a melody associated with his forbears of the clan of Ross, and the full title of the work runs: "Marche des Anciens Comtes de Ross, dédiées a leur déscendant le Général Meredith Read, Grand-Croix de l'Ordre Royal du Rédempteur"—later abbreviated to *"Marche Ecossaise sur un thème populaire."*

The work begins with a suggestion of the skirl of bagpipes, pianissimo, as though from a distance:

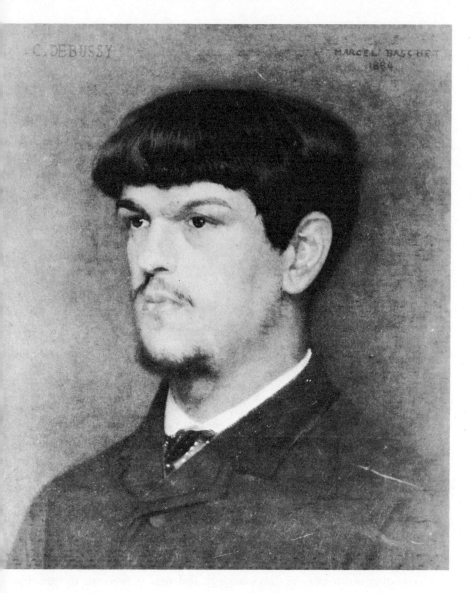

Claude Debussy (after a painting by Marcel Baschet). *The Bettmann Archive*

Little by little we seem to hear an approaching procession, until at last the theme itself makes its entrance, harmonized in modal style:

There is·a charming and quite Debussyesque middle section, derived from a variation of the theme:

This leads to a return of the theme in a quick 6/8 variation, and the work winds up with a brilliant and effective coda.

Debussy was so fond of this piece that he made his own orchestration of it, and his biographer, Léon Vallas, tells us that on hearing it for the first time many years later in 1913, he couldn't help exclaiming, "Mais, c'est joli!" It is a mystery why this work has been so neglected by orchestras and by duet pianists. Can it be that the absence of a clear return to the opening theme after the middle section gives it a slightly perfunctory air, as though Debussy didn't take the time to develop it at greater length? Or is it that pieces as short as this do not easily find a place on concert programs? Tovey has pointed out that there are a number of little masterpieces for chamber music combinations that are almost completely unknown simply because chamber music players don't seem to feel that it is worth the trouble to sit down and make music unless it is for a work of some size and substance. But it would be a pity if a work as delightful as this were to be lost to us. Perhaps at least duet pianists might make it part of an all-Debussy group, along with the "Petite Suite" and the "Epigraphes Antiques."

# XV ⁂ The French

## Florent Schmitt, Chabrier, Satie, Poulenc

Among the minor French composers around the turn of the century who made a contribution to the piano duet, Florent Schmitt deserves to be particularly noted; and if you are a French musician acquainted with his work, you may not consider him so minor. Ravel was a friend of Schmitt's from their early days at the Conservatoire, and in a letter to a friend describing a mediocre concert of contemporary music, he mentions the appearance of Schmitt on the program as follows: "In all this Schmitt sounds like an intruder; ample inspiration and melody, a splendid and capable orchestra, everything that is missing in the others." And Rowley, not to be outdone in enthusiasm, calls Schmitt's four-hand compositions "probably the finest in the whole modern repertoire."

It may be that Schmitt's music will never penetrate the borders of his native country, for he is not an innovator in any way, nor is he among those of his contemporaries like Fauré, Elgar and Rachmaninoff, whose music is equally conservative in style, but who each have their own instantly recognizable tone of voice. Schmitt's personal profile is a little elusive, and to acquire a sense for it would probably demand a more intimate acquaintance with his work than is easy to attain outside of France. But invariably his music is inventive, masterly, attractive, conceived and executed on a broad scale. Perhaps you may have a little trouble in finding some of Schmitt's larger four-hand compositions, for such things go out of print very easily, but fortunately, among the duet works of Schmitt that are still available is one unique masterpiece that you owe it to yourself to look up, the "Suite after Hans Christian Andersen," or to give it its French title, "Une semaine du petit elfe ferme l'oeil." This is another of those French suites based on the inspiration of childhood, and one of the most charming; but what makes it such a remarkable *tour de force* is the fact that the upper part is limited throughout to a range of five notes, following the educational tradition begun by Diabelli in his "Melodious Pieces." Many later composers have followed Diabelli's example for teaching purposes, but nowhere else with the extraordinary skill and imagination that Schmitt has shown here.

As the title indicates, the suite is suggested by a series of Andersen's fairy tales, in this case a series that is relatively unfamiliar to American children. The first piece, entitled "The Wedding of the Mice" is a brilliant and delightful musical picture which portrays the excited hurrying and scurrying of the mice—and here is a brief sample of the ending as they suddenly steal away. Like the entire piece, it should be played as quickly and lightly as possible:

Among the other musical pictures in this set of eight pieces are a tired grasshopper, the wooden horse of Ferme l'oeil, a curious "Promenade à travers le tableau"—a walk across the picture—and last of all, the Chinese umbrella, for which you will probably have to wait until your pupil grows up. With its crossing of hands between the parts and its sudden, unexpected rhythmical changes, it is quite difficult, and almost equally so for both players in spite of the limited range of the upper part. It would be tempting to quote from the entire set— but even better, go and get it yourself. You may have to ask your music dealer to order it from Paris, and it may take a little time, but it is well worth waiting for. If there are musical children in your family, this is an ideal piece for them, and in at least one household the copy of this work is worn and dog-eared from the joy it has given.

Schmitt has written another set of pieces in which the upper part has a five note range, "Sur les cinq doigts" published by Heugel, not quite as difficult as "Une semaine," and perhaps not quite as brilliant and original either, but still a charming set that you may like to have.

As for most of Schmitt's other four-hand music, you will have to depend on your luck at libraries and second-hand music shops. There is, however, one other duet piece of Schmitt that is available for the moment, a brilliant "Kermesse-Valse" that forms the finale to "L'Evantail de Jeanne," one of those joint musical efforts that the French, like the Russians, are so fond of. This work is a ballet that was first presented privately in 1927, composed by Schmitt, Ravel, Ibert and a number of other French composers, some of whose names are not so familiar here. As published by Salabert, it is about equally divided between numbers for piano solo and duet. Among the solos are Poulenc's delightful "Pastourelle," one of his best-known shorter pieces, a brash polka by Milhaud and an amusing rondo by Auric. Among the duets, in addition to Schmitt's, there is a delicate and characteristic sarabande by Roussel and a brilliant opening fanfare by Ravel.

Ravel's contribution is in his more "contemporary" style, and the key signature is simultaneously in B major for the right hand of the upper part, and C major for everything else, until at the very end Ravel allows them to finish together in the key of B. The piece is in a dry and witty mood that rises to a brief moment of mock-grandeur in a march with the performance indication of "Wagneramente." As Ravel's only other original contribution to the piano duet literature apart from "Ma mère l'oye," you may wish to have it as a pendant to that work.

Fauré also has written one other duet number apart from his "Dolly" suite, and as with Ravel, it is as different from it as can be imagined. This too is part of a joint composition, written together with his friend, the operetta composer, André Messager, and is entitled "Souvenirs of Bayreuth," a fantasy in the form of a quadrille, based on favorite themes from *Götterdämmerung*. We have already encountered the quadrille form in Bruckner's work, but while Bruckner's composition was entirely original, Fauré and Messager have remained more faithful to the spirit of this nineteenth-century dance, which traditionally derived its melodies from some popular stage work. Ordinarily a work of lighter character would have been chosen, and Rossini, for example, was a popular model for this type of composition. In the case of "Souvenirs de Bayreuth," the humor, of course, consists in the choice of as unlikely a work as *Götterdämmerung* for treatment in this rather frivolous dance form—and here is how the magic fire music of Wagner emerges from the treatment:

This work took its origin from an improvisation at an informal gathering in 1880, but it was not till 1930 that it was published by the firm of Costellat. Messager and Fauré have not told us who is responsible for each of the five sections of the work, and you will have to make your own guess.

This piece was to prove the inspiration for another and even more brilliant example of the same kind of musical parody, Chabrier's devilishly clever, "Souvenirs de Munich," which is based on *Tristan and Isolde*. This work too did not see the light of day till some years after Chabrier's death, when it appeared in a special supplement of a French musical magazine issued in 1911 as a memorial to him. Chabrier was the master of a light, brilliant and colorful style which struck a new note in French music, and was to be a particular inspiration for many of the French composers who came after him, Ravel and Debussy among them. But Chabrier was a major composer in his own right, and you may find in his fresh and bright style, with its sharply individual point of view, a certain affinity with the early Impressionist art of Manet, who was a particular friend of his. Chabrier had a gift of musical drollery that was particularly suited to this form of musical burlesque, and in fact he has carried it off so brilliantly as to make Fauré's and Messager's attempt seem a little tame by comparison. The humor of this music, which depends to a great extent on knowledge of the work it is based on, cannot easily be described in words, but perhaps this excerpt will give you some idea of it:

Poulenc has called this "painting a moustache and false nose on Wagner," but when you can do it with this kind of flair, then you have raised parody to the level of an art form. In spite of appearances, Chabrier's intentions were not in the least irreverent, for he adored Wagner, and indeed, it was a performance of *Tristan and Isolde* in Munich that made so overpowering an impression on Chabrier as to confirm a vague interest in a musical career into a definite determination to become a composer. This hilarious "Souvenirs de Munich" is really a token of love and affection for Wagner, in a manner possible only to a Frenchman.

The French have a certain feeling for musical humor that is entirely their own, and if you want to see to what extreme it can be carried, then you will have to turn to the work of Erik Satie. Satie was a figure out of the Paris of Toulouse-Lautrec, a complete original in both his life and his music. He made his living at night by providing piano accompaniments to the nightclub acts in the boîtes of Paris, while during the day he explored his own unique musical universe with absolute and utter incorruptibility. One of his hobbies was collecting umbrellas, and Milhaud tells of meeting him once at a street corner during a pouring rain with a closed umbrella that he refused to open because it was too valuable. On another occasion a friend—said to be Debussy—urged him to devote more attention to form in music, to which he responded by composing his "Three Pieces in the Form of a Pear." These three pieces, the earliest of his duet compositions, are still in print as published by Salabert, and you may be interested in looking into them as an introduction to Satie's style. Each of the three pieces is quite brief, but the set is introduced with a lengthy section entitled "Manière de commencement" followed by another section entitled "Prolongation du même," and the entire work is further extended by a section called "en plus" which leads to a final "Redite."

You may find Satie's music a little disconcerting at first, with its obstinate naïveté, its rhythmic monotony, its sudden bursts of thunder, and indeed, judged purely as music, it tends to be a little hollow. But it would be a mistake to judge Satie's work purely as music; it must be considered in the frame of reference of his own strange, pokerfaced humor, with its curious and far-fetched literary connotations; and then somehow it takes on its own quality of pungency, of character, and at certain moments, of a reserved yet appealing beauty.

Shortly after the composition of these three pieces in his late thirties, Satie embarked on a three-year course in composition at Vincent d'Indy's "Schola Cantorum," and the two duet collections that appeared after this rigorous training, entitled "En Habit de cheval" and "Aperçus Désagréables" show a greater musical depth and finesse. "En Habit de cheval" consists of four sections, two chorals, each only two lines long, introducing two fugues, the first entitled "Fugue litanique," the second, "Fugue de papier." Satie's far-fetched titles by the way, are apt to be quite enigmatic, and you will have to find your own interpretation of them. Here is the beginning of the first chorale, which will give you some idea of Satie's quite individual harmonic color:

The "Aperçus Désagréables" consist of a pastorale, a chorale, and a fugue—can this be a takeoff on César Franck?—and here is a moment of a grave and reserved beauty from the opening pastorale:

But when you find beauty in Satie it is likely to be only momentary. There is not too much musical sustenance in Satie, and it is a little difficult to take him seriously from a musical point of view. He does have a character entirely his own, and for certain musicians his laconic wit and his cool individual harmonic color have struck a peculiarly responsive chord. Satie has had a great influence on French music, particularly on the group of "Les Six" who considered themselves his disciples, and among them Poulenc, Milhaud and Auric have made his influence a permanent part of their musical style. Poulenc for example has been able in certain works to carry on the tradition of Satie's dry, insouciant humor, lifting it to a musical plane which Satie himself was never able to achieve. Among these works, one of the most engaging is an early sonata for piano duet, which Poulenc wrote at the age of nineteen. It is in three short movements entitled Prélude, Rustique and Finale, and you can see from the very opening notes that it is intended tongue in cheek. Listen to these massive, almost menacing chords that begin the work:

But of course Poulenc is pulling our leg, and in a few moments we can catch his friendly glance:

The slow movement is only a few lines long, and is very nearly as naive as Satie, but already it shows a mastery of pianistic color that was not in Satie's vocabulary. The "Final," marked *Très vite* alternates fragmentary reminiscences of the other movements with snatches of Poulenc's characteristic bittersweet dissonances:

The movement and the entire sonata are over before you know it. If Poulenc has his serious moments, you will not find them in this work. But this sonata, slight as it is, has a charm that remains permanently in the memory.

# Later Days

Wɪᴛʜ Satie, Poulenc and Stravinsky we have begun to approach our own time, and perhaps it might be well at this point to pick up some of the loose strands we have left elsewhere. We noticed in our chapter on Brahms that a number of his contemporaries were interested in the piano duet, but the leading composers of the following generation such as Strauss and Mahler, no doubt under the overpowering Wagnerian influence, tended to lose touch with the piano duet style and with the chamber music style in general. In Reger, however, the Germans found another master of their own to carry forward their older and more classic musical traditions.

The music of Max Reger is solidly rooted in the past, his chief influence being Brahms, along with a considerable admixture of contrapuntal tendencies inherited from Bach. Brewed together with a powerful flavoring of chromatic harmony, the result is something for which the German-speaking peoples have developed a particular taste. In Georgii's momumental survey of piano music, both solo and duet, he devotes almost an entire chapter to Reger's duet compositions, copiously supplied with musical illustrations, while the French composers of the same period, Debussy and all, have to be content with hardly more than a single page. And in *Vierhändig*, that very Germanically oriented survey of piano ensemble music, the authors refer to Reger's two-piano variations on a theme of Beethoven as "the crown of the entire two-piano literature," thus bypassing a host of things that non-German music lovers would no doubt have preferred to nominate for that honor.

But all the same, Reger is a serious and gifted composer who is well worth your attention. In some ways Reger's style is particularly well suited to the piano duet, for generally speaking his music tends toward extreme richness and fullness. As you play his piano solo music you can't help suspecting that he would have appreciated a few extra hands to help catch all the notes, and even his duet music is so thick in texture that another hand or two might still be helpful. At any rate, Reger certainly belongs in that line of composers who are more comfortable in the larger reaches of the piano duet than the piano solo, and who have contributed an unusually large share of their piano writing to it.

Reger's duet compositions begin with three sets of waltzes, opus 9, "12 Walzer Capricen," opus 10, "20 Deutsche Tänze," and opus 22, six waltzes. The later works include five "Pièces pittoresques," opus 34, six "Burlesken," opus 58, and the six pieces of opus 94, of which the last two collections are still in print and available in the Peters edition. Of the earlier waltzes, opus 20 has been reprinted by the Universal Edition, a pleasantly Brahmsian collection with just a few hints of the Reger to come, and numbers seven and seventeen of opus 10 are reprinted together by Schott, both pieces of charm and *gemüthlichkeit*.

But to savor the full quality of Reger's style, you have to go to the larger pieces of opus 58 and 94, more varied in scope, and much more characteristic of Reger's mature musical language. The six "Burlesken" of opus 58 are remarkable in that they are each in a fast tempo in much the same vein of rough unbuttoned humor, with only an occasional momentary attempt at variety of mood. Thus they can hardly be played as a set, but individually they are most interesting pieces, filled with humor and imagination. You should be warned that they are quite difficult, both in terms of the notes you have to cover and in the rapidity of harmonic change, but perhaps you might like to look into them as a new kind of musical challenge. Here is the opening of the fourth of the set of six, which will give you some inkling of their character:

The six pieces of opus 94 are more varied in mood, and are perhaps a more representative example of Reger's work. Among them are an organ-like prelude and fugue which constitute the last two numbers, a rough and vigorous waltz as the fourth number, and two impressive slow movements which are the first and third pieces of the set. As an example of Reger in his more intimate, gracious and rather Brahmsian mood, here is an excerpt from the second piece in B minor:

Like so many composers who have made a great name for themselves in their own country and not yet elsewhere, Reger is something of an acquired taste for foreigners who have the problem of seeking out a perspective that will show him in his best light. But he is an authentic composer whose music teems with ideas, harmonically, contrapuntally and pianistically. At moments he may seem a little too engrossed with his own ingenuity, and sometimes one is struck by a certain lack of flexibility in his rhythmical phrasing. But when you have finished playing one of Reger's intensely compressed and individual pieces, you will find that it has been an experience, and perhaps you may wish to look into his work more fully.

In the twentieth century Reger's most direct descendant has been Hindemith, who resembles him in his prolific mastery of every form, his sympathy for classical traditions and his interest in the piano duet. Hindemith's sonata for piano duet is one of the most interesting twentieth-century contributions to the piano duet literature, and even if you think you don't like twentieth-century music, you don't have to be shy of it, for it is not at all a forbidding work. If you listen to Hindemith's own recording of it with Jesus Marie Sanroma you will find that it is in quite a delicate and intimate chamber music style, and Hindemith might possibly have even called it a sonatina, for it is not on a particularly large scale, nor is it excessively difficult technically.

The first movement, *mässig bewegt*—moderately fast—begins simply and unaffectedly with this gracious theme in 3/4 time:

Before long it moves to what might be a second theme, a little more rhythmically active, but still marked *ruhig*—quiet. These two motives are briefly developed and intertwined before the opening theme reappears and leads, not to the second theme, but to a coda which begins with an inversion of the opening motive of the second theme in the lower part.

The next movement is a bright, glittering, rhythmically alert little scherzo, a perfect foil for the lyrical third movement which follows, the heart of the work. Here be sure to bring out the melody of the left hand of the upper part, marked *mezzoforte,* as against the *pianissimo* of the right hand:

This quiet mood is interrupted by a brilliantly pianistic *sehr lebhaft* section in 9/8 time, which sounds as if it were going to be a finale, but turns out instead to be only a middle section as Hindemith returns to the opening theme of the movement to end the entire work on a peaceful note.

Hindemith has moved away from Reger's hyper-chromatic style into a contemporary idiom of freer atonality, which at the same time seems oriented toward a key center, particularly as each movement comes to an end. Notice how delicately the key center is defined as the chords ending the first movement seem to hover around and finally settle toward the key of C:

The scherzo ends with this delicate and charming alternation of the chords of B flat and C sharp minor:

And here is the ending of the last movement, as the key center of E major is affirmed, almost as an afterthought, yet with perfect inevitability:

This sonata, written in 1936, may be considered the last of the long line of classic sonatas for piano duet beginning with J. C. Bach and Mozart, and it forms a beautiful and fitting end to the series. Hindemith has sometimes been called by his more enthusiastic admirers the Bach or the Beethoven of this century—but perhaps it may not be invidious to suggest rather that he is the Telemann of our time, a greatly gifted and prolific composer who has enriched every area of the repertory, whose mastery is always extroverted and intelligent, and whose rhythmic sense is always inventive and alive.

Turning from the German to the Italian composers of this century, we will find that although they have not been overly productive in the field of the piano duet, they have still left a few things well worth looking into. Respighi, for example, has written a piano duet suite for beginners dating from 1926 that is one of the most charming works of its kind composed in this century. Respighi's extraordinary gift for instrumental color finds its best expression in his orchestral music, but even in terms of the piano duet his sensitive feeling for instrumental timbre can assert itself, as in this delightful bell effect from the "Christmas Song":

The other pieces of the suite include a gently sentimental "Romanza," a Sicilian hunting song, an Armenian melody and two Scottish numbers, an air and a Highland fling. This little suite published by Rahter is still in print, and is one of the most attractive works available for beginners.

Casella too has left a few things for piano duet, some of which he later scored for orchestra. Perhaps you might like to look up his "Puppazetti" or Marionettes, a charming suite, again not too difficult, that exploits some of the modernistic devices of the twenties. Here is an example of his delicate use of polytonality:

Speaking of Italian composers for the piano, we could hardly omit the brilliant and intellectual Busoni, who has made a greater name, perhaps, as a pianist and musical thinker than as a composer. Yet his music still arouses interest, and continues to attract its own adherents, among whom is the eminent British pianist, John Ogden, who has recorded the monumental piano concerto. In spite of Busoni's avant-garde interests and contacts, he is not at all a modernist in his compositions; his music is solidly based on nineteenth-century harmonic procedures, and suggests nothing so much as a kind of wayward Mahler. For piano duet, Busoni has left a set of two "Finnish Dances," which date from a two-year stay in Finland, and which are a worthy addition to the long series of national dances for piano duet beginning with Brahms' "Hungarian Dances" and Dvorak's "Slavonic Dances." These two pieces, published by Peters, are powerful and individual works of a rather serious and somber cast, that are well worth studying and playing.

It is curious that the English, who with Carlton and Tompkins in the seventeenth century and Burney in the eighteenth were the very first to explore the possibilities of the keyboard duet, have left so little for the medium since then. The first flicker of activity in the piano duet after those halcyon days came in the mid-nineteenth century with Sir William Sterndale Bennett, a talented adherent of the Leipzig school and the leading English composer of his day. Bennett's music has disappeared from the repertory, unless we except a revival here and there at some occasional festival of Romantic music, but all the same it is possible to discern an individual profile in it once you know it well enough to discount the all-pervading Mendelssohnian influence of his time. Bennett has left one duet composition, a set of three "Diversions," opus 17, which you can find at the Library of Congress in Washington, and which might very well prove worthy of performance, particularly the charming and graceful middle movement of the set.

At the turn of the century when English music experienced its first genuine renaissance since the golden days of the sixteenth and seventeenth centuries, its leading exponents were such choral and orchestral masters as Elgar, Delius and Vaughan-Williams, who composed next to nothing for piano, let alone piano duet. But among the lesser

British composers of this century, one of the few who have taken an interest in the piano duet is that original and eccentric humorist, almost a kind of English Satie, Lord Berners. Like Satie, Berners was gifted with an exquisite sense of the ridiculous which found expression in an imaginative use of titles and a gift for unconventional musical illustration, and like Satie again, Lord Berners found the piano duet a congenial medium for his musical thought. Berners' three "Valses Bourgeoises" comprising a "Valse caprice," a "Valse brilliante" and "Strauss, Strauss et Strauss" show him in a characteristic mood, and this brief excerpt from the last piece of the set may give you an idea of his humor:

Berners has made piano-duet versions of two of his orchestral compositions, a suite of "Trois Morceaux" and a "Fantasie Espagnole" in three movements, both published by J. and W. Chester of London.

In somewhat the same vein of slight but clever musical illustration is Allan Rawsthorne's suite of pieces entitled "The Creel" after Sir Izaak Walton. These four little pieces, each of them a musical interpretation of one of the sea species of Walton's "The Compleat Angler" are only a page long apiece, marked by a delicate musical whimsy expressed in terms of the most idiomatic piano writing.

Another oddity of twentieth-century English duet music, in this case evoked by the sixteenth century, is Peter Warlock's "Capriol Suite," a series of free arrangements of the musical illustrations found in Arbeau's "Orchesography," the earliest dance manual extant. Peter Warlock has taken these dance tunes of an earlier period and developed them in his own way, keeping much of their archaic flavor while adding occasional suggestions of twentieth-century harmony. This work, originally written for string orchestra and adapted for piano duet by

. the composer, is a delightful thing that deserves to be better known than it is.

Like the English, the Americans were interested in the duet medium from its beginnings in the eighteenth century, if we may judge from the unusually rich collection of the very earliest printed duet music in original editions at the Library of Congress in Washington. There is however no original duet music of any importance by native American composers until the period just preceding the Civil War when that brilliant and original composer-pianist of New Orleans, Louis Moreau Gottschalk came upon the scene, dazzling music lovers of both Europe and America with his virtuosity. In his own lifetime, and for a little while after, Gottschalk's charming and extremely pianistic salon pieces were immensely popular in this country, but they have, of course, long since faded from the repertory. Quite recently, however, there has been a renewed interest in Gottschalk's music, not only for its period flavor, but for its pioneering use of native American and South American melodies and rhythms, and the pieces that have been resurrected have proved remarkably worthy of revival. Along with his numerous solo pieces, Gottschalk has left a little collection of duet music which, although not in print at the moment, can be found in the three major collections of Gottschalk's music in American libraries, that of the Library of Congress, the New York Public Library and the Sibley collection in Rochester.

The first American composer after the Civil War to achieve anything like an international eminence was Edward MacDowell, a fine pianist as well as a sensitive composer, who is still best remembered for his piano music. MacDowell left two collections of duet pieces, opus 20 and 21, of which the latter, entitled "Moon Pictures" is still in print as published by Schirmer's, and you could do much worse than to look into it and study it. It is a relatively early work, not quite as characteristic as his later things, but the five pieces that make up the set, based on Hans Christian Andersen's "Picture Book without Pictures" have a modest grace and charm of their own. It must be admitted that to some degree this music is a little dated; no doubt the "Hindoo Maiden" of the opening piece would be more at home in a turn of the century drawing room than the plains of India, and the bears of the final "Bear Dance" are remarkably tame and well mannered. But in "The Swan," the finest piece of the collection, you can find something of the crystalline clarity of MacDowell's later piano writing:

The work as a whole is not at all difficult, and might very well be studied by moderately advanced students. It still retains its appeal, and it can help give us a better-rounded picture of MacDowell than we are likely to get from the familiar *Woodland Idylls,* or an occasional hearing of the Second Piano Concerto.

After MacDowell there is something of a hiatus in American duet music until recent decades when the duet medium has experienced a considerable and surprising renewal of activity. The dean of contemporary American composers, Samuel Barber, who occupies a place in present-day American music somewhat analogous to MacDowell's in his own time, has composed a charming set of pieces for piano duet entitled "Souvenirs," opus 28. Barber tells us that it is intended as a period piece, and asks us to imagine ourselves in the ballroom of a fashionable hotel in the period just before the First World War. The dances that comprise the set include a waltz, schottische, two-step, Hesitation Tango and galop, to which is added a "Pas de Deux" as a kind of slow movement. All these dances are filled with a nostalgic, bittersweet flavor redolent of the period, and perhaps a brief quotation from the "Pas de Deux" will suggest something of their mood, evoking, like a faded snapshot, the era of our parents and grandparents.

Somewhat comparable in its use of the dance forms of another time
and place is the "Dance Suite" of Robert Kurka, an extremely talented
American composer who died prematurely in 1957. The dances of
Kurka's suite are a Furiant, Polka and Waltz to which are added a
Prelude and Finale to round them out, and if Barber's dances evoke a
recent American past, Kurka's suggest the atmosphere of the Central
Europe of his own Czech antecedents. Where Barber suggests a sophisticated hot-house atmosphere, Kurka recalls the open spaces of
the Bohemian fields; his music is fresh and cool, even slightly astrin-
gent in quality. Here is an excerpt from the Polka, characteristic of
Kurka's out-of-doors feeling:

This suite is not at all easy, but with its natural freshness and spontaneity, you will find it well worth learning and playing.

Among other American composers who have written serious and
ambitious compositions for piano duet are Wallingford Riegger, some
of whose powerful and vigorous pieces have been published by the
Peer Music Company; Harold Shapero, who has a fine sonata in a
Stravinskian style published by Schirmer's, and Vincent Perischetti,
whose "Concerto" for piano four hands is in the Elkan-Vogel catalogue.

In the area of four-hand teaching pieces for children, a particularly
valuable contribution has been made by Norman Dello Joio, who has
written two collections of children's pieces, originally for his own
family, of which the first, "A Child's Day" is on an extremely simple
level, charmingly illustrating a child's activities from playtime to
bedtime. No doubt Mr. Dello Joio's children have done very well at the
piano, for his next set of pieces is on a considerably more advanced
level; these too are musical and well written, and will give much
pleasure to any musical child. Another little teaching piece of great
charm at about the same level of difficulty is the "Child in the Garden"

by Alan Hovhaness, a greatly gifted American composer whose beguiling musical style reveals in this quasi-Oriental idiom Hovhaness' interest in his Armenian heritage.

No doubt a very great impetus to the production of four-hand music in this country in recent years has been provided by the activity of a number of enterprising four-hand teams who have not only played American compositions, but who have actively commissioned them, notable among them being the husband and wife duos of the Salkinds, the Wentworths and the Freundlichs. Among the many interesting compositions that we owe to this source, one of the finest is the "Fantasie Concertante" by that gifted and versatile Austrian-Israeli and now American composer, Robert Starer. This work makes no concessions whatever in terms of pianistic difficulty—it is frankly a demanding work of almost symphonic range and scope. But for advanced players who are looking for something challenging and stimulating, this is something they can sink their teeth into. Starer has also written a set of "Five Duets for Young Pianists" that are fortunately much more accessible to students. There are no compromises here either; the level of musical integrity is the same, and it demands serious attention, although on a less advanced level. But for those students capable of tackling it, it is one of the most rewarding of teaching collections.

The piano duet team of Milton and Peggy Salkind has been extremely active in commissioning new music and the list of composers who have produced works for them includes such names as Seymour Shifrin, Ben Weber and Ralph Shapey, all of them serious and dedicated musicians who write in a very contemporary style, with a strong tendency in a serial direction. The Salkinds have even commissioned from the talented California composer, Andrew Imbrie, that rarity of rarieties, a concerto for piano duet and orchestra, one of the very few of its kind since Czerny.

If the taste of the Salkinds runs to a contemporary twelve-tone style, the Wentworths, Kenneth and Jean, have gone a step further in encouraging avant-garde experiments in the medium of the piano duet. They are responsible for some of the most remarkable and unique piano duet compositions in existence. Characteristic of them is Joel Spiegelman's "Morsels," published by the MCA Music Corporation. Spiegelman has had to resort to a number of innovations in notation in order to indicate to the performers some of the experimental devices and techniques that he calls upon them to use, including such things as tapping the piano strings with the fingers, or asking for the strings to be lightly muted on the harmonic. We have grown accustomed to a variety of experiments in the unconventional use of the piano in John Cage's well-publicized compositions—but the application of these techniques to the piano duet seems to open up entirely new possibilities. Indeed, it may be that the piano duet is the natural goal for this kind of piano writing, for it adds enormously to the possibilities in unconventional uses of the piano when two people rather than one are available to help manage them. A soloist is terribly limited when it comes to treating and adapting the piano, but with a second pianist available, it now becomes possible for one of the partners to devote himself to adjusting the piano, or working on effects with the piano strings, while the other is free to work at the keyboard. The potentialities are multiplied so enormously that it may be that what John Cage has done with a single pianist is only a start compared to the possibilities inherent in the piano-duet medium.

If the musical values represented by such a piece as "Morsels" prove to have a permanent validity, then we may be at the beginning of an entirely new cycle in the history of the piano duet. Certainly these developments are in an embryonic stage at the moment, but who knows what the future may bring?

⊞ *Epilogue*

I$_N$ the preceding chapters we have covered a great range and variety of material. But of course we haven't covered everything; and in fact one of the attractions of the duet medium is the room it leaves for your own discoveries. Music goes out of print all too easily, and nothing more easily than piano duet music. Certainly it is strange that a little masterpiece like Debussy's "Marche écossaise" should not be available. But why not make a virtue out of necessity and become your own musicologist? If you can't buy this delightful piece at a shop, and if you can't order it, at least you can find it in the reference room of the New York Public Library; and thanks to the Xerox process you can obtain copies of anything you wish, not only in American libraries, but in libraries throughout the world. Or if you have played the three duet sonatas of J. C. Bach that are in print and would like to look up more, all you have to do is refer to Terry's excellent biography of the composer * which lists not only J. C. Bach's complete works, but every library that owns them. Thus you will find that there are two additional duet sonatas that were printed in Bach's lifetime and have never been reprinted since. They are in the music room of the British Museum, and if you request it, they will most courteously arrange to Xerox them and send them to you. Of course it takes time, but if you have a little patience a few more weeks won't make that much difference, and then you will have your own copy of the two duet sonatas of J. C. Bach not included in the Peters Edition. Perhaps you may agree that the editor has chosen the best of the sonatas to reprint, although certainly the finale of the D major sonata is equal to them.

If you'd like to go a step further, you might even write to the library at Brussels for J. C. Bach's six early duet sonatas or "lessons" that were never published at all and exist only in manuscript. Then you can make up your own mind as to whether they are good enough to be

---

* Try to get the second edition, which is more correct and complete than the first.

genuine or not, a point on which some musicologists have expressed reservations. And while you're at it, you might notice that the catalogue of Christian Bach's works includes a few other interesting curiosities; how about a sonata for harp and piano, for example, in case you know a harpist you might like to try it with.

Actually, the amount of duet music in print is something like the tip of the proverbial iceberg, only a very small fraction of the whole, and whether it is entirely the best fraction is an interesting question to investigate. Perhaps you might like to look into other periods of musical history along with J. C. Bach or Debussy. The three marches by Alkan, opus 40, which you can find at the Library of Congress in Washington, are fascinating things if you have the technique to perform them, and if you care for this period and this composer. Incidentally, Alkan is just beginning to have a revival of his own, largely due to the efforts of Raymond Lewenthal who has issued an excellent collection of his solo music, and if you share in the interest and enthusiasm that Alkan has begun to inspire in some musical circles, you can participate yourself in the rediscovery of his work.

Certainly one of the advantages of the piano duet medium is the opportunity it gives you to get to know the masters in greater depth than would otherwise be possible. And for some of the minor masters it may be the only way you can get to know them at all. In this connection, do not neglect the duet arrangements of symphonic music that were so popular in the last century. Even with the tremendous proliferation of recordings of all kinds in recent years, there are still certain areas of music that you can get to know only on your own, and sometimes only with the help of the piano duet. For example, Raff's *Leonora Symphony* is a splendid work in its own way which does not even exist in recording, but the piano duet arrangement of this symphony and of other Raff symphonies can still be found in some of the second-hand music shops in New York and elsewhere, and on the shelves of music libraries.

It is curious that among painters the minor masters are still given the respect they deserve, whereas in music any composer who has not remained "on top of the greased pole," among the handful of the supreme masters, is likely to be neglected, if not scorned. Certainly a painter of a stature comparable to Raff's would command high prices at the auction galleries and be accorded an honored place in the museums. But Raff is out of print, not even recorded, and has become hardly more than a footnote in music history. Yet the *Leonora Symphony* is still a splendid work, imbued with a noble spirit and filled with a profusion of beauties. Raff, by the way, has very much his own style, but if you notice a touch of MacDowell in such a turn of phrase as the following:

it is because MacDowell studied with Raff and picked up some of his mannerisms. Or perhaps you might like to look into the other of the two musical R's, Rubinstein, who left five symphonies, which if you are to get to know them at all, will be only through the medium of the piano duet. The best remembered is the *Ocean Symphony,* of which the composer was so fond that he added a second slow movement and scherzo to it after it was finished, leaving to conductors the option of choosing which of the two slow movements or scherzi they wished to include. If you play over the piano duet arrangement of the *Ocean Symphony,* you may find to your surprise that it is a vastly pleasing work. Or speaking of Russian composers, perhaps you may like to look up Taniev, the "Russian Brahms," so highly regarded by every musician who knew him and studied with him. His first symphony in its duet arrangement is on the open shelves of the New York Public Library, and it is your only chance of getting to know it. Or Glazunov's symphonies, if you have a taste for that period. Or Spohr's chamber music. Or to go back a little, to original duet music again, Dussek has written a series of piano duet sonatas which some musicians rate higher than the solo sonatas, but while the solo sonatas have all been reprinted the duet sonatas have hardly been touched as yet. Fortunately, the Library of Congress has an excellent collection of Dussek's duet sonatas in their original editions, and if you look up the sonata in B flat, opus 74, for example, you will find that it is a little masterpiece, not unworthy to stand beside Haydn and Mozart.

However, aside from the fascination of exploring the bypaths of musical history that the piano duet makes possible, it would be hard to exaggerate the inestimable benefits it can afford you as a musician. Where else can you find such a sure method for learning to keep in time? Or learning to count measures? Or where else will you find a better opportunity to develop your skill as a sight reader? Or to acquire the rough and ready of practical music-making—that is, to "fake"? And most important, how better can you learn the art of listening to your neighbor as well as yourself, which is the alpha and omega of all ensemble music?

During the course of this book we have ocassionally offered hints in regard to the performance of certain compositions, and perhaps at this point it might be fitting to offer a few general suggestions in regard to playing duets. First and foremost, to repeat, and it can't be repeated too often, learn to listen to your partner as well as yourself. Don't be a soloist! And at the same time, don't be an accompanist either, for both parts of the music have equal importance—with the one proviso, however, that as in piano solo music, or in any music at all, the melody must sing. If you neglect that, either as soloist or as duettist, it is the beginning of all flat and boring playing. This is something, of course, that is rarely indicated in the music, but if you will look at such a passage as the beginning of the slow movement of Schubert's "Grand Duo," you will find that this theme loses all its beauty and meaning unless the melody clearly stands out above the accompaniment as though given forth by a voice, or, if you prefer, an oboe:

Only then will the magical grace of this exquisite theme be apparent.

Of course, as a corollary to this, it is extremely important for the lower player to know how to limit his volume. We have just remarked that you mustn't be an accompanist, but all the same, the lower range of the piano has a natural tendency to sound louder in proportion than the upper, and the secondo player must learn to develop a particular tact in handling the sonority of the bass. And since, of course, all pianos differ in this respect, he will always have to be alert.

If the lower player doesn't usually get to play the melody as much as his partner, at least by way of compensation he usually handles the pedal, for he is in a better position to judge the harmony and to gauge the necessity for using the pedal. But there is no hard and fast rule about this, and sometimes you may wish to change around and give the upper player a chance at it. Then he will have to be particularly careful to listen to the lower part, and even to glance sometimes across the page to his partner's music. As a matter of fact, a roving eye is a useful trait for a duettist to possess, for it will often be desirable to glance momentarily at your partner's music to get a better idea of what is going on, and you will have to learn to do it without losing your own place. Naturally, this is a little easier when the two parts are printed together on the same page one below the other, and occasionally you will find the music printed this way. Composers first have to write their music this way in any case, and since most experienced duettists prefer this method of notation, it is to be hoped that some day this practice will be followed in printed music as a matter of course.

One last point: it is well to remember that duet playing is not primarily a medium for the concert stage. Like all chamber music, and perhaps even more so, its natural habitat is the home rather than the concert platform, and often it can be a mistake to try to carry over the style of the concert stage into the piano duet medium. Bear in mind that finesse is less important than spontaneity. You are playing for yourself rather than for an audience; if you have listeners they are there by courtesy, and your music should not be so much heard as overheard.

And yet in spite of the difficulties and hazards of public performance of duet music, it is remarkable how in recent years a number of four-hand teams have overcome the obstacles to successfully playing duets in public, and have made places for themselves on the concert stage and in the record catalogues. Artur Schnabel and his son, Karl-Ulrich, were among the first, and they have left some fine records of Schubert and others. More recently two first-rate artists, Karl Demus and Paul Badura-Skoda, who have both made names for themselves as solo pianists have joined together in four-hand music with excellent results. If you will listen to their recording of the Schubert "Grand Duo," you will find it a model of the skill and artistry that can be applied to the performance of piano duets. You may not agree with all their tempos;

perhaps the opening movement might have attained a greater sense of relaxation with a more moderate tempo, and even the slow movement might perhaps have been taken a shade slower. But all the same it captures the Schubertian magic, and that is the important thing. On the other hand, they take the finale much nearer to *allegro moderato* than to the *allegro vivace* that Schubert has marked, and yet it comes off perfectly at their tempo. Curiously enough, Joachim in transcribing this work for orchestra has actually changed Schubert's tempo mark to *allegro moderato,* although in this case one might have supposed it to be in consideration for the problems of orchestral handling. In any case, the finale in the Demus-Badura-Skoda performance is filled with masterful interpretive touches that come off perfectly at their chosen tempo, which has the added advantage of leaving a little room to speed up later. Perhaps you might like to compare their Schubert interpretations with those of another talented duet team, Milton and Peggy Salkind, who have also done much recording. Their approach is different in many respects, but it has a freedom and spontaneity that is of the essence in the duet style.

By now, in fact, enough duet recordings have appeared to enable you to form a collection of your own, with room for a number of different interpretations of some of the classics of the medium, such as the Schubert "Grand Duo" and Fantasy in F minor. And in contemporary music, perhaps you may like to look up the work of Kenneth and Jean Wentworth, who have made the avant-garde something of their own special province, and who have achieved masterful results in works of this genre, many of which they have commissioned themselves.

But however much you listen to duet performances, and collect recordings, remember that the chief delight of the piano duet medium lies in playing it yourself. Through it you can develop your own skill and musicianship, and through it you can enjoy the companionship of another musician, who may perhaps throw new light on your own musical ideas. And through it too you may find the opportunity of exploring uncharted musical seas, and of making unexpected musical discoveries.

# 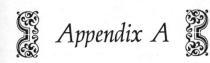 Appendix A  A Note on the Two Piano Literature

If you have a second piano, then the entire literature of two-piano music is open to you, a literature quite different in style and character from that of the piano duet. While the two piano literature is not quite as broad or rich as that of the piano duet, there are some wonderful things in it, and generally speaking it is more familiar than the duet repertory since there are a number of active and excellent two-piano teams who have concertized and recorded extensively, whereas piano duettists in general have preferred to limit themselves to the more intimate confines of the home. The two-piano literature has been explored in depth in Hans Moldenhauer's excellent monograph entitled *Duo-Pianism*—but for convenience we are sketching a brief outline of some of the high points of the repertory.

As with the piano duet, the history of the two-piano medium begins with Mozart and a few of his contemporaries and immediate predecessors.* The sons of Bach, apart from Johann Christian, were more interested in two-keyboard music than in duets for one instrument, and Wilhelm Friedemann has left three works for two claviers, while Carl Philip Emanuel has a set of four duettos. Even Johann Christian composed a two-piano work that supplements his more numerous duet compositions, a sonata in G major in his best style, available through Schott.

The first two-piano masterpiece that has remained in the repertory is Mozart's brilliant and delightful sonata in D, K. 448, a work in his most sparkling *galant* vein that remains one of the peaks of the two-piano literature. Mozart's two-piano output also includes a splendid fugue in C minor, as well as an unfinished andante and allegro that has been completed by Paul Badura-Skoda and published by Schirmer's. Among Mozart's contemporaries, Clementi has left two sonatas for two pianos, both in B flat and both in his best style, and the catalogue of Dussek also includes a few two-piano compositions, unfortunately not in print.

* If you are interested in the few isolated examples of two-keyboard compositions dating from the earlier days of the harpsichord, Moldenhauer has a chapter on them in which he reprints in full a piece by Giles Farnaby entitled "For Two Virginals" and an "Alemande" of François Couperin.

There is something of a hiatus in the two-piano literature during the time of Beethoven and Schubert, but the line continues again with the Romantics of the 1830's and 40's. Schumann's lovely set of variations in B flat, opus 46, is another of the high-water marks of the two-piano literature, even though it was first written with an obbligato of two cellos and French horn which were later discarded. We have mentioned the Mendelssohn-Moscheles variations on a theme of Weber in its piano-duet form, but the two-piano version is more brilliant and slightly more extended. Moscheles was particularly fond of this medium, and first made his reputation as a composer with his two piano "Hommage à Handel." Liszt, in addition to arranging his symphonic poems for two pianos—a more congenial medium for him than the duet versions he also made—has left a very interesting Concerto Pathétique for two pianos that deserves to be better known. Chopin's only composition for two pianos is an exquisite early rondo in C, published posthumously as opus 73.

Among the great masters, Brahms is the chief contributor to the two-piano medium with his splendid two-piano sonata opus 34bis, an early form of the work that later became the piano quintet in F minor, and his variations on a theme of Haydn, opus 74bis, again the first form of what was to become one of his greatest orchestral works. Unfortunately we no longer have the two-piano version of Brahms' opus 15 which he destroyed after turning it into his first piano concerto, but we do have Brahms' own arrangement for two pianos of his third and fourth symphonies, as well as a set of five waltzes taken from his opus 39, which he put into this form for his friend, Karl Tausig. A word of mention is due Grieg for his two piano "Variations on an old Norwegian Melody" and for his second piano parts to four of Mozart's piano sonatas. Reger was particularly fond of piano-ensemble music, and in addition to his piano duets left an interesting but extremely difficult set of variations for two pianos on a theme of Beethoven as well as arrangements for two pianos of his organ introduction, passecaglia and fugue, and his orchestral variations on a theme of Mozart.

The French composers have contributed a number of masterpieces to the two-piano medium, notable among them being Saint-Saëns, whose brilliant variations on a theme of Beethoven are only the best known of a number of compositions for two pianos. Chabrier's "Trois Valses Romantiques" are perfect gems, each one of them, and Debussy's "En blanc et noir" is one of the finest of his later works.

Among Russian two-piano compositions, the delicious waltz from Arensky's first suite is one of the best known, but Arensky has written five suites in all. Rachmaninoff's two suites are among his finest compositions, the second in particular, which was written at the same time as the second piano concerto, and is in no way inferior to it.

In our own time the two-piano medium has flourished as the piano duet has languished, and the list of contemporary composers who have contributed to it is an impressive one. Noteworthy among them are Stravinsky, whose "Concerto per due Pianoforti soli" and "Sonata for two pianos" are among his boldest and most uncompromising works, and Bartok, whose sonata for two pianos and percussion is one of his masterpieces. Hindemith has written a most interesting sonata for two pianos, and among the most popular of twentieth-century two-piano compositions is Milhaud's brash and witty suite, "Scaramouche." Many recent English composers have written for two pianos, among them Vaughan-Williams with a fine "Prelude and Fugue" and Britten with his "Introduction and Rondo Burlesca." The list of American two-piano compositions is long, including works by such varied composers as Aaron Copland, Paul Bowles, John Cage, Norman Dello Joio, Morton Gould and a host of others.

It is not surprising that composers have found the two-piano form a more satisfactory medium for treatment with orchestra than the piano duet, and if we go back to the days of the harpsichord, then we can begin the list of concertos for two keyboards with Bach, who left no less than three. Two of them, both in C minor, are transcriptions of concertos for solo instruments, but the other, a fresh and vigorous work in C major, was originally conceived for two harpsichords and orchestra. The two harpsichords are virtually complete in themselves, and do not call for an orchestra at all in the middle movement, and in this sense we can very well say that the literature for two keyboards begins with Bach. Among Bach's sons, both Wilhelm Friedemann and Carl Philip Emanuel left concertos for two keyboards and orchestra.

Mozart's charming and witty concerto in E flat for two pianos is one of the most delightful works in the medium, and among Mozart's contemporaries, Dussek also has a two-piano concerto, not yet republished. In the nineteenth century, Mendelssohn left two very early but quite playable concertos, and perhaps we might include Saint-Saëns, whose "Carnival of the Animals" is in some of its movements virtually a two-piano concerto. In the twentieth century the list of concertos for two pianos and orchestra has grown enormously, and without trying to include everything, we might at least mention the two-piano concertos of Poulenc, Martinu, Milhaud, Arthur Bliss and Roy Harris, as well as Bartók's own concerto version of his sonata for two pianos and percussion.

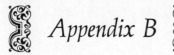 

*Chapter III. The Early Days: J. C. Bach and Mozart*

If you would like to study the Carlton and Tompkins pieces as they were first written, you can find them reprinted in their entirety in their original form as part of a very interesting article entitled "The Earliest Keyboard Duets" by Hugh M. Miller, which appears in the *Musical Quarterly* for October, 1943. The Schott version is edited with an introduction by Frank Dawes, and is entitled "Two Elizabethan Duets."

The sonata by Burney in Douglas Townsend's anthology is supplemented by another of Burney's sonatas issued separately by Alec Rowley in the Schott edition. Burney published his duet sonatas in two sets of four each, and if you are curious about the others, you can find them in the New York Music Library and in the Music Division of the Library of Congress in Washington. Douglas Townsend's collection also includes a pleasant but rather lightweight "Duettino" by Tomasso Giordani, a "Divertimento" by Johann André and a fine sonata by Clementi as well as Haydn's complete duet compositions, the "Partita" and "Master and Scholar," both of which include a minuet as a second movement.

Johann Christian Bach's three sonatas are readily available in the Peters edition. Two others, not reprinted since the eighteenth century are available at the Library of Congress or the British Museum. J. C. Bach also wrote a set of six "lessons" which can be found only in a manuscript copy at the Brussels *Conservatoire Royal de Musique*. They are shorter and simpler than the sonatas, and may have been intended for teaching purposes, but if they are not up to the level of the Peters sonatas, they still contain some interesting things. For a moment in the finale of the fifth of the series, J. C. Bach reminds us that he is the son of the great Sebastian:

Although Johann Christian's two greatly talented brothers, Wilhelm Friedemann and Carl Philip Emanuel left works for two claviers, they both ignored the medium of the piano duet. However, the fourth of the Bach composer brothers, Johann Christoph Friedrich, known as the Brückeburg Bach, did compose two sonatas for piano duet, of which one in A major has been reprinted by the firm of Otto Heinrich Noetzel Verlag, and is available through the Peters edition office in New York. If J. C. F. Bach is not a composer quite on the level of his three brothers, this two-movement sonata is still a fine work, and well worth having if you are interested in this period. While Johann Christian Bach has an affinity with Mozart, Friedrich Bach is closer to Haydn, although he still has his own individual profile. If you would like to get better acquainted with him, then look up a collection entitled *The Joy of Bach* for piano solo, edited by Denes Agay and put out by the Consolidated Music Publishers of New York. It is an anthology of easy pieces by Bach and his four sons in which Friedrich is given equal representation with his three better-known brothers. His music stands up very well against theirs, and each of his pieces in the collection is masterfully written, alert and inventive.

It is curious that Bach's line, in spite of his numerous progeny, died out in the third generation with his last grandson, Wilhelm Friedrich Ernst Bach, the son of Friedrich Bach. W. F. E. Bach was also a composer, not a professional like his father or his uncles, but a talented amateur, and one of his pieces is reprinted by Schott, a charming little andante in A minor that shows something of the influence of Mozart in his more romantic vein. Schott has coupled this piece, under the title "Zwo Stücke für Vier Hände" with a sonata by a little-known contemporary of Bach's sons, Ernest Wilhelm Wolf, interesting historically as one of the earliest of duet sonatas, but of negligible interest musically. Among other lesser-known composers of the period, Schott has also reprinted two sonatas by one Johannes A. Just, who is almost completely lost to fame, not even being listed in Grove or any other reference work. However, these two sonatas are agreeable and well written, and might very well be used as teaching pieces. Also valuable as teaching material are a set of "Tonstücke" by Daniel Gottlob Türk, published by Schott in two volumes. Türk was one of the most interesting composers of his period, and his music has lost none of its value.

Naturally you will have no trouble in getting Mozart's duet compositions, and your only problem will be to decide among the various publishers. Perhaps the best choice is the Henle-Verlag, since in addition to all the standard works included in the other editions, it also contains the boyhood sonata in C, K.19d, as well as the unfinished sonata in G.

Clementi is also easily available, the six duet sonatas of his opus 14 and 16 being collected together in one volume by Schirmer's, while the remaining sonata from opus 6 is included in a Schirmer classic duet anthology. Schirmer's has also issued three rondos by Clementi, which are Clementi's own four-hand arrangement of movements from various chamber-music works.

Dussek's three sonatinas, opus 67, available from the Elkan-Vogel Company of Philadelphia, are worth having, although they are not as fine as the larger duet sonatas, of which the Library of Congress in Washington fortunately has an excellent collection. A sonata in G minor by Pleyel is published by Peters, as is a divertimento in A minor by André. Summy-Birchard has also issued a set of six sonatinas by André, edited by Goldberger and Zeitlin, which are useful as teaching pieces. A few other items of the period may be found in various duet anthologies of the early and classic periods, issued by a number of publishers.

If you are further interested in the historical aspects of the early period of the duet, then you might look into Walter Georgii's *Klaviermusik,* which is published in German by the Atlantis Verlag of Zurich. Georgii is very thorough and enumerates everything available. Among the earliest of eighteenth-century duets are an unpublished sonata by Nicola Jomelli, dating before 1774, a routine example of the style of the period, and a set of three sonatas by Christoph Heinrich Müller published in 1782, which are at the Library of Congress in Washington. Also from this period, at the Library of Congress, is an imaginative sonata, opus 6, by Franz Benda as well as sonatas by Leopold Kozeluch, Theodore Smith and others. Among the numerous figures mentioned in Georgii, perhaps the most interesting are Christian Neefe who was the teacher of Beethoven, J. W. Rust who enjoyed a brief moment of fame a century after his death as a result of d'Indy's interest in him, and Johann Wilhelm Hässler, a truly fine talent whose sonata in C minor might well be revived.

## Chapter IV. Beethoven

Beethoven's chief four-hand compositions, the sonata opus 6, the three marches and the two sets of variations are published together in a great variety of editions. The "Grosse Fuge," however, is included only in the Henle-Verlag edition, and for some reason or other this volume is difficult to obtain in the United States. If you can't get it, at least you can Xerox the "Grosse Fuge" from the complete edition of Beethoven's works, which is available at any large music library. There is a gavotte for four hands dating from Beethoven's boyhood, which Harold Bauer has edited for Schirmer's, and although it has little of the mature Bethoven about it, it is still rather charming in a large eighteenth-century fashion. A few spurious Beethoven four-hand compositions have turned up occasionally, most recently a set of six German Dances, reprinted by Peters from an unsigned manuscript and quite gratuitously attributed to Beethoven, although they are without any spark of Beethoven, or indeed, any musical spark whatever.

Czerny's "Sonatine Brillante," edited by Douglas Townsend, is published

by Sam Fox, Inc., and is well worth having as a teaching piece. The Newberry Library in Chicago has an unusually rich collection of Czerny's music,
and is probably the best source of his interesting output for piano six hands.
Of the six pieces for three pianists at one keyboard published under the
general title of "Les Pianistes Associés," the Newberry Library possesses opus
229, "Divertissement Militaire," opus 295, "Variations on an air from Bellini's
*I Montechi e Capuletti,"* and opus 297, "Variations on an air from *Norma."*
They also have a number of excerpts from the six-hand collection, opus 609,
"Les Trois Soeurs," although the numerous pieces that make up this set
are trifling pot-boilers for beginners, routinely arranged from familiar folk
songs and melodies of other composers. The New York Music Library and
the music division of the Library of Congress also have good collections of
Czerny that can provide more of his four- and six-hand music.

Ries' duet music is not easy to come by, but the New York Music Library
has a set of four-hand variations on a theme of Rossini, and the Library
of Congress has the four-hand variations on a national air of Moore. Fortunately Diabelli's four-hand music is kept in print by many publishers, and
you will have no difficulty in obtaining it. Schirmer's publishes his opus 149,
"Twenty-eight Melodious Pieces on Five Notes," the easiest of the sets, and
one of the best beginner's introductions to four-hand music. "The Pleasures
of Youth," opus 163, is a little more difficult, but also very valuable, and
Schirmer's puts out a collection of five charming sonatinas, two from opus
24, and opuses 54, 58 and 60.

As for Hummel, you will again have to seek in the libraries, but he is
still quite well represented. The New York Library has the two sonatas, opus
51 and 92, the nocturne, opus 91, and the "Valses, suivies d'une bataille," as
well as an early and charmingly Mozartean "Rondeau agréable" in G. There
is also a set of variations on a Tyrolean air by Hummel in the Schirmer's
collection of "Eleven Piano Duets" edited by Zeitlin and Goldberger. To
Hummel's credit also are his arrangements of Beethoven's symphonies which
first made them familiar to nineteenth-century households.

### Chapters V, VI and VII. Schubert

The complete collection of Schubert's four-hand music as put out in three
volumes by Peters, Schirmer's and International Editions, or in five volumes
by the Kalmus Edition are all quite satisfactory. However, if you are interested
in having the three early fantasies, then you must get the Henle-Verlag edition, also in three volumes, or the Dover reprint of the Breitkopf and Härtel
complete edition in which the duet compositions are compressed into one
large volume. The Henle edition is the only one that contains the two
supplementary ländler in G and E, both charming pieces that came to light
in this century, and that are issued individually by Schirmer's. The firm of

Schott has published a separate volume of Schubert's waltzes for four hands that includes these two ländler, the four ländler of 1824 that are in most of the standard editions and two four-hand excerpts from the waltzes opus 33 as well as a set of eleven ländler arranged by Brahms for four hands. If you are curious about the four-hand version of the entire set of waltzes of opus 33, then you will have to seek out a copy of the old Litolff edition, and you will need a little luck to find it.

The overture in F, opus 34, is found in most editions, but the two early overtures in the Italian style in C and D are found only in the Henle edition and in the Dover reprint of Brietkopf and Härtel. One piece that is curiously enough missing from all the standard editions including Henle is the overture in G minor, one of the most attractive of the group of four. It was omitted from the Brietkopf and Härtel edition simply through oversight, but it did find a place in the supplementary volume 18 of the complete edition, so if you want it, you will have to buy a copy of the Dover reprint of this volume of Schubert's complete works. But if you do, you will have as a bonus Schubert's own duet transcription of his *Fierrebras* overture, as well as a variety of interesting miscellaneous or unfinished compositions for piano solo.

### Chapter VIII. Weber and Mendelssohn

Of course you won't have any trouble in finding the standard duet works of Weber and Mendelssohn, which are in the catalogues of a number of publishers. Weber also has two brief but charming waltzes for four hands that are included in a set of "Twenty Dances" published in the Kalmus edition. The duet arrangements of the Mendelssohn overtures are rather hard to come by now, but the English firm of Augener still lists them in its catalogue. Among them Mendelssohn is responsible for the duet version of the overture to the early *singspiel*, "Son and Stranger," as well as to the *Midsummer Night's Dream*.

The Mendelssohn-Moscheles variations on a theme of Weber can be found in their duet form at the Library of Congress in Washington. Of Moscheles' numerous duet compositions, the sonata in E flat, opus 47, is on the open shelves of the New York Public Library, while the Boston Public Library has a few additional things, including the "Daily Studies," opus 107, based on the scales in all the keys for one player, with free variations for the other. Perhaps this work might be worth sampling as a way of easing the loneliness of scale practice, even if you may not have the patience to work out all twenty-four of them. Moscheles also wrote a suite for eight hands at two pianos, "Les Contrasts" opus 115, which is in the New York Music Library. Among other duet works of the earlier romantic period, the Boston Library has two fine sonatas by George Onslow, which are attractive works that might well be dusted off and given a hearing again.

## Chapter IX. *Schumann*

Schumann's complete piano duets are published by Peters and the International Music Company, and you might as well have them all. The "Bilder aus Osten" and the "Twelve Children's Pieces" are also published separately by a number of firms.

As for the early polonaises, if you can't find a second hand copy anywhere, you will probably have to apply to the New York Public Library or the Library of Congress in Washington to have your own Xerox copies made. Perhaps you might also like to look up Schumann's "Spanische Liederbuch" which contains two interludes for piano duet.

Certainly among the most tantalizing of all the lost musical compositions of history are a set of four-hand variations by Schumann on a theme of Prince Louis Ferdinand, which date from the same year as the early polonaises. Prince Louis Ferdinand, a nephew of King Frederick the Great, was a musical amateur of unusual gifts whose compositions were highly esteemed in his day, and which might very well prove worthy of revival. Schumann once called him a romantic before his time, and a full-length study of this remarkable man and his music is certainly overdue.

## Chapter X. *Brahms*

Brahms' duet music is of course all in print, but you will have to buy each of the compositions separately since they they have never been published together in a single volume.

Brahms' great rival symphonist, Anton Bruckner, is also represented in the publisher's catalogues by a set of teaching pieces which he wrote in his early years for his pupils, and by a quadrille for duet. But these works have absolutely nothing of the stamp of the greater Bruckner about them, and are not even interesting enough to be particularly useful as teaching pieces, so you might as well save your acquaintance with him for the later symphonies and choral works, where he comes into his own.

Among the other of Brahms' contemporaries discussed in this chapter, Moszkowski is the only one whose duet music has the distinction of having remained in print, and his "Spanish Dances," opus 12 are so pleasant and so grateful pianistically that you really should have them.

Apart from the Goetz sonata which is to be found in the New York Music Library, most of the other works discussed in this chapter are available at the Library of Congress. Among other composers of this period, Max Bruch wrote an early Capriccio for piano duet, opus 2, an attractive piece that might well be revived—but for this you will have to apply to the British Museum. And certainly we should add a word of mention for such typically nineteenth-century curiosities as Ferdinand Hiller's "Operette ohne Text" and Felix Draeske's "Nutcracker and Mouse King." The Hiller work is, as its title suggests, a duet composition following the form of an opera with overture, arias, recitatives and so on, but without a text; and the Draeske work is an elaborate musical retelling of the fairy tale. Both these works are by respected and prolific composers, but somehow this kind of extravagance seems to belong to the nineteenth century, and it is not likely that it will escape from it.

If you would like to look further into this period, then Georgii is as always thorough and conscientious, and takes up as sympathetically as possible a number of additional minor figures.

## Chapter XI. Chopin, Liszt and others

The firm of Edward B. Marks which has published Chopin's early "Variations on a National Air of Moore" has also issued a facsimile reproduction of the Chopin manuscript with an introductory article which provides much interesting data on the composition.

None of Liszt's duet music is in print, and you will have to apply to a variety of libraries if you want to obtain the works mentioned in this chapter. The Göllereich biography which includes the "Fest-Polonaise" as part of its musical supplement is at the New York Music Library, the "Christmas Tree Suite" is at the Library of Congress in Washington, while the Boston Public Library has the duet version of the "Galop Chromatique" and the duet arrangement of Field's Nocturnes. The "Valse de Bravura" in its duet version can be found only at the Columbia University Music Library.

Incidentally, the variation on Chopsticks which both Raebe and Searle list as a duet piece is only a trifle of a few bars for piano solo which is reproduced in a facsimile of Liszt's manuscript in the Boosey and Hawkes edition of the "Paraphrases on Chopsticks" by four Russian composers. The Notturno in F sharp listed in Searle's catalogue as a duet piece is there by mistake, for after the publication of this catalogue Mr. Searle noted that this work is an arrangement of the Petrarch sonnet 104 made by Gottschalg and not Liszt himself. Liszt's own duet arrangement of "Les Preludes" is published by Schirmer's, but for the duet versions of the other symphonic poems as well as the various other duet arrangements in the Raabe and Searle catalogues, you will have to trust to luck in second-hand music shops and libraries.

Field's duet compositions must also be sought out at various libraries; the "Variations on a Russian Air" and the "Grande Valse" in A are in various collections, but the Rondo in G can be found only at the library of the Royal College of Music in London. Alkan is even more elusive than Field in American and British libraries, for only his three marches, opus 40, are in the Library of Congress, but perhaps you may have better luck with the other works in French libraries. Of the other Alkan duets listed by Rowley, the "Fantasy on Don Juan" is an enormously difficult bravura piece, while the "Final" in D minor is much more playable, if you can find it. Alkan also published the finale of his cello sonata, opus 47, separately as a brilliant duet piece entitled "Saltarelle." Wagner's polonaise, opus 2, is included in a four-hand anthology entitled "Meister der Romantik," number 4531 in the Peters catalogue. Keep an eye out for Douglas Townsend's edition of Donizetti's duet sonatas when it appears, for it should be a welcome addition to any collection.

## Chapter XII. *Grieg and Dvorak*

Grieg's "Norwegian Dances" and "Valses-Caprices" are published by Peters, but his other duet compositions may be harder to come by. Incidentally, Grieg made duet arrangements himself of his "Peer Gynt" music and his incidental music to "Sigurd Jorsalfur," opus 22, his two "Elegiac Melodies" opus 34 and "Two Norwegian Melodies" opus 64 for strings, and the "Norwegian Bridal Procession," opus 19, number 2 for piano solo.

Among other Scandinavian composers, Gade has left an attractive set of three marches for piano duet which are at the Music Library of Columbia University, and Christian Sinding wrote a number of duet compositions, of which you might like to look up his "Six Pieces," opus 35, published by Peters.

Dvorak's "Slavonic Dances" and "Legends" are issued by a number of publishers, but for the suite, "From the Bohemian Forests" you will have to apply to the Czech publishing house, Artia. Peters also publishes a polonaise in E flat, written originally for orchestra in 1879, but available only in its duet version. Dvorak's piano "Silhouettes" opus 8 and "Ecossaises" opus 41 were also issued simultaneously in duet verions, which are now long out of print.

The catalogue of Dvorak's great Czech contemporary, Smetana, includes nothing for duet, although he wrote an allegro in E minor and a rondo in C for eight hands at two pianos.

## Chapter XIII. *The Russians*

Tschaikowsky's folk song arrangements are issued by many publishers, and Rachmaninoff's "Six Pieces," opus 11, are available from the International Music Edition. Fortunately the complete "Paraphrases" by Borodin, Rimsky-Korsakoff, Cui and Liadov have been reissued by Boosey and Hawkes, along with a manuscript facsimile of a brief contribution by Liszt for piano solo, and a less interesting supplement by a minor Russian composer named Scherbachev.

Glinka's duet compositions are collected into one volume by the Russian Publishing House, available in America from Leeds, and the firm of Jurgenson has published the "Capriccio" separately with a Polka in F not included in the Russian edition. As a kind of pendant to the "Paraphrases," you might like to investigate a little tarantella by Glinka's contemporary, Dragomijsky, in which the second pianist plays nothing but a pedal point E in broken octaves. Perhaps this charming piece, which is at both the New York Music Library and the Library of Congress, may have first given Borodin the idea for his polka on chopsticks. Its second part can easily be played by a single hand, and so it might form with the "Paraphrases" and Stravinsky's "Three Easy Pieces" a slim literature of three handed music. Stravinsky's two collections of "Easy Duet Pieces" were originally published by Chester, but they appear in a number of anthologies, including Erno Balogh's "Eighteen Duet Pieces" published by Schirmer's.

## Chapter XIV. The French I

Fortunately, most of the music we have discussed in this chaper is in print and readily available. The Bizet and Fauré suites are in the catalogue of the International Edition as well as in French editions. Ravel's suite, "Ma mère l'oye" and Debussy's two sets of duet pieces are in the Durand edition and very much in print, although rather on the expensive side. You may have to look a little harder for Debussy's "Marche Ecossaise," but at least it is in the New York Public Library where you can readily have Xerox copies made.

As a matter of historical curiosity, a purported early symphony in B minor in one movement of Debussy, written while he was in the service of Mme von Meck and existing only in a four-hand version, has turned up recently in Russia and has been reprinted by the Russian State Publishing House. It is available at the Boston Public Library, but is of very little interest, being strictly a student exercise without any trace of Debussy's future gifts. Perhaps you may be interested rather in Debussy's own four-hand arrangement of "La Mer" and "L'après-midi d'un faune," although these works are so perfectly conceived for orchestra that they necessarily lose much in an arrangement, even Debussy's own. It is not likely that your dealer has them in stock, but no doubt he can get them for you from Paris if you wish to order them. Ravel has undertaken the even more impossible task of arranging his own "Bolero" for piano duet as well as for two pianos, and has done an amazing job of transferring that essentially orchestral work into a pianistic framework. With each succeeding return of the theme Ravel adds some slight touch of pianistic color until, as in the orchestral version, he has imperceptibly attained a tremendous climax at the end. If you didn't know it as an orchestral work, you might almost have imagined that it was written for the piano. This remarkable *tour de force* is still in print and can be ordered from the catalogue of Durand.

## Chapter XV. The French II

Luckily Florent Schmitt's "La semaine du petit elfe" is in print, if you can wait patiently while your dealer orders it from Durand in Paris. His "Sur les cinq doigts" is also available, in this case from Heugel. Also published by Heugel is "L'Evantail de Jeanne" which is worth owning in its entirety, although like most imported editions, you will find it rather on the expensive side. Fauré's and Messager's "Souvenir de Bayreuth" was available in Paris in 1966 from the Editions Costellat, and Chabrier's even more amusing "Souvenir de Munich," also published by Costellat is listed in the catalogue of the Associated Music Publishers, although it is an open question whether you will find it in stock. As a last resort, you may have to fall back on the New York Music Library.

Satie's "Trois pièces en forme d'une poire" is still in print at the Editions Salabert, 22 rue Chauchat, Paris 9, but the other two collections will have to be uncovered in second-hand shops or libraries. Fortunately Chester has kept Poulenc's delightful four-hand sonata available, and you will have no trouble getting it. Among other members of "Les Six" Milhaud has two duet works in his characteristically bright and astringent style, which work excellently for duet even though both are arrangements; a set of three "Enfantines" arranged from settings of Jean Cocteau, and the "Suite Provençale" based on French folk songs, originally written for band. Auric's catalogue includes "Chandelles romaines," and a set of five "Bagatelles," very much in the style of his movie music, cool, dry and sophisticated.

There is a great variety of other recent French four-hand music that is well worth having, but it is always a toss-up whether it will still be in print or not. You may wish to refer to Alec Rowley's little handbook on four-hand music for his excellent and quite full listing of French duets, although you will first have to find that in the library, for that too is out of print! Rowley's book was prepared in the 1940's, and of course much music that might have been available to him then in England may have disappeared by now. However, that is all part of the fascination and adventure of being a four-hand aficionado, so keep up the search through dealers, second hand shops and libraries, and you may come up with more than you expected.

Florent Schmitt's four-hand music apart from his five-finger exercises may not be among the easiest things to find, but they are worth looking for. Along with them, you might keep in mind another five-finger study that is almost as clever as Schmitt's—perhaps in its own way even cleverer—André Caplet's amusing "Un petit tas de choses," published by Durand in 1925. Caplet, unlike Schmitt, has limited himself to a five-finger position on the white keys only, but he has allowed his more difficult secondo part to travel into a variety of other keys, complete with their own key signature. However, this music is not at all far out, or even polytonal; Caplet simply harmonizes his melodies in such a way that the upper pianist can keep in tune with the foreign keys without using sharps or flats. A brief excerpt from the first piece of the set, a berceuse in D flat, will give you some idea of his method:

Among other works for student and teacher, Roger Ducasse's interesting "Studies" are worth looking into, although after the first few pieces even the upper part becomes almost as difficult as the lower. Roger Ducasse's earlier "Petite Suite" is charming, and perhaps more practical for piano duettists. Another interesting and not too difficult four-hand suite is by none other than Raoul Bardac, the little brother of Fauré's· "Dolly," who turned out to be something of a composer himself. His "Petite suite majeure," published by Durand in 1914, is a charming work by a talented amateur. And perhaps you might like to look into another fairy-tale suite, "Images pour les contes du temps passé" by Claude Delvincourt, published by Alphonse Leduc. Among the fairy tales that Delvincourt has provided images for are the sleeping beauty and "Le petit poucet," both entirely different from Ravel's treatment of the same fairy tales, but attractive in their own right.

Most valuable for children are the five volumes of Ingelbrecht's "La Nursery," a series of duet settings of French children's songs. In these pieces the upper part is of quite moderate difficulty, while the lower part, although a little more complicated, is still easily manageable. Ingelbrecht was a well-known composer and conductor in the early years of this century, and these pieces are all turned out with the utmost grace and charm, and cannot be too highly recommended. Somewhat more difficult, but filled with a delicate refinement and musical inventiveness are four "French Sonatinas" by Charles Koechlin, published by the Oxford University Press. Koechlin was a favorite pupil of Fauré who was entrusted with the orchestration of his master's lovely "Pelléas et Melisande" Suite.

Among other things that Rowley lists are three sets of duets by Reynaldo Hahn, an intimate friend of Proust, and a most talented composer of salon songs. Particularly tantalizing in Rowley's listing are two sets of duets by one P. Dupin, whose name is unknown even to Grove. But Rowley comments on these works: "Without rushing into superlatives, we may describe these pieces as 'utterly delicious'." May you have luck in finding them.

And certainly it would not be fair to leave France without mentioning that hardy and durable master of the French Biedermeyer style, Saint-Saëns, on whom critics are not accustomed to spending much time, but whose music continues to flourish in the repertory, giving pleasure to performers and listeners alike. Only one of Saint-Saëns' duet pieces is available in America, a gay and witty "Pas redoublé," which is included in Erno Balogh's anthology of *Eighteen Piano Duets* published by Schirmer's. But Rowley lists three compositions, and the complete Saint-Saëns catalogue in Grove lists five, all published by Durand, and you might want to look for them when you are in France.

## Chapter XVI. Later Days

Reger's major duet compositions, the "Burlesken," opus 58, and the "Six Pieces," opus 94, are both available in the Peters edition, and the six waltzes of opus 22 are now published in the Universal edition. Reger has also made duet arrangements of Bach's six Brandenburg concertos and four orchestral suites which are published by the International Music Company. Hindemith's duet sonata is of course available from Schott. Incidentally, Hindemith himself has made the duet arrangement of his symphony, "Mathis der Maler," published by the Associated Music Publishers. Among other later German duet compositions, a charming set of five Christmas songs by Hermann Schroeder is published in the Schott edition, and Walter Gieseking's amusing duet piece, "Spiel um ein Kinderlied," published by Johannes Oertel, sometimes turns up in music shops.

Busoni's "Finnish Dances" in the Peters edition, and Respighi's six pieces in the Rahter edition are still available, but unfortunately Casella's interesting duet music may not be so easy to find. In addition to the easier "Puppazetti," Chester has also published a more ambitious, impressionistic set of duet pieces entitled, "Pagine di Guerra" which are well worth having if you can find them. Chester is also the publisher of Lord Berners' amusing duet collection while Peter Warlock's delightful "Capriol Suite" is issued by J. Curwen and Sons. Rawsthorne's "Creel Suite" is published by the Oxford University Press, as are William Walton's duets for children.

In addition to the Gottschalk duet collections at the New York Music Library and the Library of Congress, you may be interested in watching for a complete reprinting of Gottschalk's entire piano works, including the duets, by the Arno Press, 229 West 43 Street in New York. In case you would care to look further into MacDowell's duet music, his collection of "Moon Pictures," opus 20, is at the Columbia University Music Library and may be obtained in Xerox copies from them. Among American duet compositions dating from the early years of the twentieth century are a set of three folksy "American Dances" by Henry F. Gilbert, published by the Boston Music Company, and a set of attractive Birthday Waltzes, opus 2, by the distinguished writer on music, Daniel Gregory Mason.

Among the compositions discussed in this chapter, the Barber "Souvenirs" are published by Schirmer's, the delightful suite by Robert Kurka is available from the Weintraub Music Company in New York, while Starer's "Fantasia Concertante" and teaching pieces are both published by the MCA Music

Company. The teaching pieces of Dello Joio are published by Marks, and Hovanhess' "Child in the Garden" is in the Peters catalogue. Douglas Townsend, whose pioneering editorial work we have often referred to in these pages is also represented in the Peters edition by a set of four inventive "Fantasies on American Folk Songs," and among other American composers whose duet music is in print are Ernst Bacon, whose work is published by Lawson-Gould and the American Music Edition; Eugene Hemmer, who has an interesting set of pieces in the Spire edition of Cincinnati, and Sam Raphling, whose clever set of teaching pieces entitled "Two Plus Two" is published by the General Music Company of New York. Worth looking into also are sonatas by Ernst Toch and Bernard Heiden, both in the Associated Music Publishers catalogue.

Obviously it would be impossible to attempt anything approaching a complete list of contemporary American duet music. If you keep track of the publishers' catalogues and follow the activities of such duet teams as the Salkinds and the Wentworths, you will be struck by the flourishing state of duet music at the present time. Both the Salkinds and the Wentworths have even commissioned that rarest of all musical forms, the concerto for piano duet, the Salkinds from Andrew Imbrie, and the Wentworths from William Sydeman, who has transformed his "Concerto for Piano Four Hands and Chamber Orchestra" of 1967 into a "Concerto for Piano Four Hands and Tape" of 1969. If you count the classic example of Czerny, and the more recent example by the contemporary English composer, Malcolm Arnold, that doubles the number of duet concertos to four.

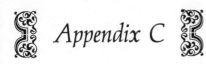 *Appendix C* 　 *Duet Material for Beginning Pianists*

One of the values of the piano duet is its usefulness from an educational point of view—in teaching time and rhythm, for example, and ensemble playing. There is a very sizable catalogue of teaching material for duet, and while much of it is undistinguished and routine, there are a number of things by the great masters that should be known to teachers.

In addition to the brief list that follows, there are occasional excerpts from larger and more difficult works that can be used very profitably by beginners. The opening Pavane of Ravel's "Mother Goose" suite, for example, is as simple as it is lovely, and the same might be said of the first piece of Fauré's "Dolly" suite. There are also some movements of the sonatas of Mozart and J. C. Bach that can be attempted too. Schubert is less useful for beginners, however; even the little "Kindermarsch" that he wrote especially for the young son of some friends is not really too easy, and you had better save Schubert till later.

Easiest of all are some of the pieces in the following collections, in which the pupil's part is limited to a range of five notes:

Anton Diabelli—"Melodious Pieces on Five Notes," opus 149
　An excellent introduction to duet playing; the pupil's part is on an extremely elementary level in the opening pieces.
Anton Diabelli—"Pleasure of Youth. Six Sonatinas on Five Notes," opus 163
　A little more difficult, but still very useful.
Florent Schmitt—"Sur les cinq doigts." (Heugel)
　Not difficult and quite attractive
Florent Schmitt—"La semaine du petit elfe ferme l'oeil" (Durand)
　Not as easy as the above, but delightful material for a talented youngster.
Godowsky—"Twenty Pieces on Five Notes" (Carl Fischer)
　These are useful too, with rather sophisticated parts for the teacher.

Other pieces in this category that are worth having, although they may require some looking for, are César Cui's "Ten Pieces on Five Notes," Reinecke's set of twelve pieces, and André Caplet's "Un petit tas de choses."

Among collections in which the pupil's part is easier than the teacher's, although not limited to five notes, the following are particularly attractive.

Tschaikowsky—"50 Russian Folk Songs"
A delightful set, not too difficult for either part.

Ingelbrecht—"La Nursery" (Editions Salabert, Paris)
Based on French folk songs, most tastefully and charmingly arranged.

Stravinsky—"Five Pieces" (easy right hand)
Stravinksy—"Three Pieces" (easy left hand)
Both these collections appear in a number of anthologies, including the Schirmer's publication, *Eighteen Piano Duets* edited by Erno Balogh. They are very interesting, but will usually require an adult beginner to handle even the pupil's part.

Norman Dello Joio—"Family Album" (Marks)
Very easy and quite attractive little pieces.

Milhaud—"Enfantines" (Editions Max Eschig, Paris)
Worth having for pupils who might like to try something more contemporary.

The following collections are of about the same level of difficulty for both parts, and can be used very profitably by two students as well as teacher and pupil.

Haydn—"Master and Scholar"
This amusing teaching piece has always been a hardy perennial, and is reprinted in many collections.

D. G. Türk—"Tonstücke" (Schott)
By one of the earliest pioneers of the piano duet, this collection still retains its interest and charm.

Schumann—"Twelve Pieces for Young and Old Children," opus 85.
This beautiful work is the classic among teaching pieces for duet, but it is not quite as easy as the "Album for the Young" and must be reserved for students who are a little more advanced.

Schubert-Brahms—"Eleven Ländler" (Schott)
Charming waltzes by Schubert that have been considerably simplified in Brahms' arrangement as a result of being divided between two players.

Arensky—"Six Children's Pieces," opus 34 (International Music Edition)
Not difficult, and very attractive.

Gretchaninoff—"On the Green Meadow," opus 99 (Leeds)
Very valuable as one of the very easiest among the teaching collections listed.

Respighi—"Six Pieces" (Rahter, available through Associated Music Publishers)
These charming and euphonious pieces deserve to be much better known than they are.

Alexandre Tansman—"Les jeunes au piano" (Editions Max Eschig, Paris)
In four volumes, of which the first, "En tournant la T.S.F." is the easiest, this is a valuable addition to the teaching repertoire.

William Walton—"Duets for Children" (Oxford University Press)
Slightly more contemporary than the above collections, this is a useful supplement to them.

Robert Starer—"Five Duets for Young Pianists" (MCA Music)
For more advanced beginners, these interesting pieces will be most stimulating.

# Index of Compositions Covered

All the compositions mentioned or discussed in this book, whether in the body of the text or in the supplement, are listed here by composer. Two-piano compositions mentioned in Appendix B are included along with piano duet compositions, but are printed in italics to differentiate them more easily.

Fantasia in F minor, K. 594, 20–21
Fantasia in F minor, K. 608, 20–21
*Fugue in C minor, K. 426,* 189
Fugue in G minor, K. 401, 18
Sonata in B flat, K. 538 (186c), 13
Sonata in C, K. 19d, 12, 193, (Mus. Ex., 12)
Sonata in C, K. 521, 11, 13, 16, (Mus. Ex., 11)
Sonata in D, K. 381 (123a), 13, (Mus. Ex., 13)
*Sonata in D, K. 448,* 189
Sonata in F, K. 497, 13, (Mus. Ex., 14–16)
Sonata in G (unfinished), K. 357 (497a), 16–17, 193, (Mus. Ex., 17–18)
Variations in G., K. 501, 18
MULLER, CHRISTOPH HEINRICH
3 Sonatas, 194
NEEFE, CHRISTIAN
Duets, 197
ONSLOW, GEORGE
Sonatas in E minor and F minor, 196
PERISCHETTI, VINCENT
Concerto for piano four hands, 180
PLEYEL, IGNAZ
Sonata in G minor, 23, 194
POULENC, FRANCIS
*Concerto for two pianos,* 191
Sonata, 167–69, 201, (Mus. Ex., 167, 169)
QUILTER, ROGER
3 English Dances, 103
RACHMANINOFF, SERGEI
6 Pieces, opus 11, 142–43, 199
*Suites for two pianos,* 142, 190
RAFF, JOACHIM
Leonora Symphony (duet arr.), 184–85, (Mus. Ex., 185)
8 Pieces, 105
RAPHLING, SAM
Two by Two, 204
RAVEL, MAURICE
Bolero (arr. by composer), 200
Fanfare from "L'Eventail de Jeanne," 163, 201
Ma mère l'oye, 6, 151–54, 200, 205, (Mus. Ex., 152–54)
RAWSTHORNE, ALLAN
The Creel, 177, 203

REGER, MAX
6 Burlesken, opus 58, 171, 203, (Mus. Ex., 171)
20 Deutsche Tänze, opus 10, 171
*Passacaglia and Fugue* (arr. by composer), 190
6 Pieces, opus 94, 171–72, 203, (Mus. Ex., 172)
5 Pièces pittoresques, opus, 34, 171
*Variations on a theme of Beethoven,* 190
*Variations on a theme of Mozart* (arr. by composer), 190
12 Walzer-Capricen, opus 9, 171
6 Waltzes, opus 22, 171, 203
REINECKE, CARL
12 Pieces on five notes, 205
RESPIGHI, OTTORINO
6 Pieces, 175, 203, 206, (Mus. Ex., 175)
RHEINBERGER, JOSEPH
Sonata in C minor, 103
RIEGGER, WALLINGFORD
Duets, 180
RIES, FERDINAND
Variations on a national air of Moore, 33–34, 195
Variations on a theme of Rossini, 195
RIMSKY-KORSAKOFF, NICHOLAS
Paraphrases, 138–41, 199, (Mus. Ex., 140)
ROSSINI, GIOACCHINO
Marches, 120
ROUSSEL, HENRI
Sarabande from "L'Eventail de Jeanne," 163, 201
RUBINSTEIN, ANTON
Bal Costumé, 104
Ocean Symphony (duet arr.), 185
Sonata, 103–104, (Mus. Ex., 104)
RUST, J. W.
Duets, 194
SAINT-SAENS, CAMILLE
Pas redoublé, 202–203
*Variations on a theme of Beethoven,* 190
SATIE, ERIK
Aperçus Désagréables, 166–67, 201, (Mus. Ex., 167)
En Habit de cheval, 166, 201, (Mus. Ex., 166)
3 Pièces en forme d'une poire, 166, 201

# General Index

# Related Paperback Books from Da Capo Press

**THE ART OF ACCOMPANYING AND COACHING**
By Kurt Adler

**THE CASTRATI IN OPERA**
By Angus Heriot

**AN ENCYCLOPEDIA OF THE VIOLIN**
By Alberto Bachmann

**GREATNESS IN MUSIC**
By Alfred Einstein

**MUSICAL WIND INSTRUMENTS**
By Adam Carse

**MUSIC AT YOUR FINGERTIPS**
By Ruth Slenczynska
With the collaboration of Ann M. Lingg

**SCHOENBERG AND HIS SCHOOL**
By René Leibowitz

**STRAVINSKY IN THE THEATRE**
Edited and with an introduction by Minna Lederman

*...available at your bookstore*